40 half in the Serrania de Ronda and Jimena area

CW00853103

Patrick Elvin

64 walks from 1.5 to 5 hours between Ronda and Jimena, based on the villages of Jimena, San Pablo, Gaucin, Colmenar, Benarraba, Genalguacil, Algatocin, Benalauria, Benadalid, Atajate, Jimera, Alpandeire and Farajan

DISCLAIMER

The author and publisher have tried to make the information in this book as accurate as possible . However information can change and we can accept no responsiblity for any loss , inconvenience or injury sustained whilst using this book.

We welcome any feedback regarding any changes or difficulties you may encounter whilst using this book .

robertpatrickelvin@gmail.com

Cover picture: Peñon de Benadalid (walks 54 and 55)

I LIST OF WALKS (numbers continue from previous book WALKS AROUND GAUCIN))

WALKS 51 – 56 GENALGUACIL/ BENALAURIA/ BENADALID

WALKS 57 -61 ATAJATE/ JIMERA AND UPPER GENAL

NOTE The numbering starts at 22 to avoid confusion with my book WALKS AROUND GAUCIN (Published by Amazon) as the numbering for Gaucin walks has been coordinated in conjunction with the town hall.

All walks in this book are different from those in my first book

MAP FOR WALKS 22 to 26

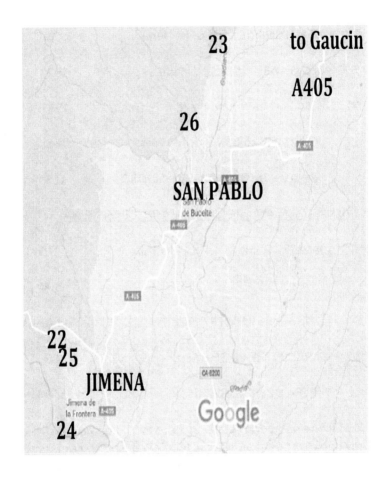

MAP FOR WALKS 27 TO 39 and 45 to 48

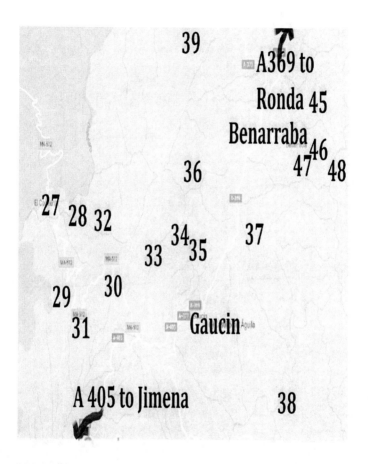

MAP FOR WALKS 40 to 44 and 49 to 53

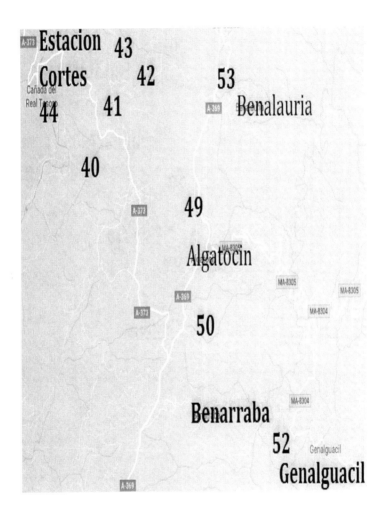

MAP FOR WALKS 54 to 61

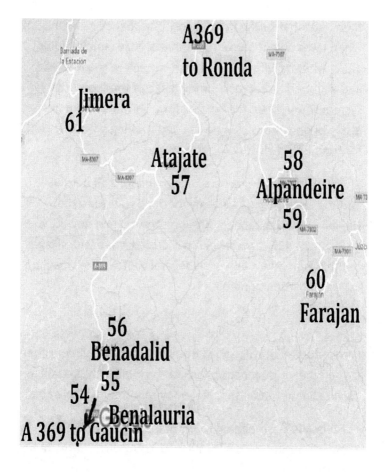

ii THE AUTHOR

I first came to Gaucin in 1976 to visit my parents and since then had a hankering to live here. The chance came in 1997 when I was able to move to a country finca (smallholding) along with my wife. I soon began to explore the local area and acquired an extensive knowledge of the footpath system throughout the whole of the Serrania De Ronda , also working as a walking guide and running a walking club for friends and visitors.

These walks are the result of a demand for half day walks and the setting up of a weekly morning walk, based on Gaucin but has extended 30 kilometres up and down the A369 and A 405 respectively to include most of the villages of the Genal valley as well as several walks in the Guadiaro valley and around Jimena.

I am indebted to colleagues from the walking club for proof testing the written instructions for the walks, thus enabling local residents and visitors to enjoy this great walking area.

This book is a companion to my first publication " Walks Around Gaucin " also published by AMAZON. There are no repeats !!

iii THE BOOK AND HOW TO USE IT

The book is a no frills practical guide to 40 diverse walks in the area of the Serrania de Ronda and extending south to Jimena, including three rivers, the Genal, Guadiaro and the Hozgarganta. It contains for each walk, brief statistics and description, how to get there, usually two maps and a profile, and Lat and Long references at key points of the walk using decimal degrees from Google Earth .(to check go to TOOLS then options then 3D view then check the show lat and long box is ticked under decimal degrees) The maps are pdf downloads from http://www.juntadeandalucia.es/institutodeestadisticaycartografia/lineav2/web and are at scale 1:10000. The numbers I have added along the routes drawn on the maps refer to key moments during the walk.

The other maps show distances in kilometres during the walk and come from www.mapometer.com and can all be found on that website and uploaded to your device. The background is google earth . Just type in the title of the walk under search or use the weblink I have placed below the map .

Most walks also have wikiloc tracks and my gratitude goes to Matthew Wolfman and Roger Collinson for these contributions: where available I have added the wikiloc link. These are downloadable free of charge to your device from wikilocs.

COMBINING WALKS TO MAKE DAY WALKS

For those who would like to do longer walks, you can combine two or more walks to make walks of between 3 and 6 hours. Several walks start in the same place and others start close to each other. Possibilities include:

Walk 22 and 25: Start walk 22 and at Map 5 turn right to join walk 25 near start (4 hours)

Walk 23 and 26: Start walk 23 and at Map 7 continue on main track arriving at walk 26 map 4 . Complete 26 and start walk 26 and at Map 4 turn right rather than left and rejoin walk 23 at Map 7 turning right at this point (4.5 hours)

Walk 25 and 24 : Start walk 25 and at Map 3 take the longer way whch leads to the start of walk 24. Do walk 24 as far as between Map 3 and 4 then leave walk 24 to join walk 25 at Map 5 (4 hours)

Walk 28 and 32: Start walk 28 ; leave walk 28 at Map 4 to join walk 32 between Map 9 and 10 (4.5 hours) Finish walk 32 at Map 8.

Walk 31 and 29 Start walk 31 and at Map 10 join walk 29 at the start , continue walk 31 at finish of walk 29 (4 hours)

Walk 32 and 33: Walk 32 at finish is start of walk 33 (5 hours)

Walk 33 and 34 :   Start walk 33 at Map 5 turn right to join walk 34 at   Map 7/8   At finish of walk 34, start walk 34 and at Map 6 on walk 34 turn right to rejoin walk 33 after Map 5 (3 .5 Hours)

Walk 35 and 36 : Start walk 35 and at Map 4 join walk 36 at Map 3 (3 hours)

Walk 39 and 40: Start walk 39 and at Map 3 join walk 40 at Map 4; leave walk 40 at Map 3 and rejoin walk 39 at Map 4 (4 hours)

Walk 39 and 44: Start walk 39; at Map 2 continue on track and join walk 44 at Map 1 . Leave walk 44 at Map 1 rejoin walk 39 at Map 2 (turn left up the hill rather than right) (4 hours)

Walk 40 and 44: Start walk 40; at Map 5 turn left to join walk 44 at map 1 . By the green painted house rejoin walk 40 at Map 6.

Walks 40,41 and 43: Start walk 40 ; after Map 6 turn left at path instead of right to join Walk 41 between Map 1 and 2 and at Map 5 join walk 43 at Map 1 (5 hours)

Walk 41 and 43: Walk 41 and walk 43 have the same start point so make an nice figure of 8 (3.5 hours)

<u>Walk 45 and 47:</u> Walks 45 and 47 have the same start point so will make a figure of 8 (4 hours)

<u>Walks 45, 46 and 47:</u> Start walk 46 and at Map 6 join walk 45 at Map 2 and at the finish do walk 47 which has the same start and finish point (5 hours)

<u>Walk 45 and 50</u> Start walk 45 and at Map 3 join walk 50 at Map 3 . Complete walk 50 and do first part of walk 50 as far as Map 3 .Rejoin walk 45 at Map 3 and complete walk 45 . (4 hours)

<u>Walk 47 and 48:</u> Start walk 47 and at Map 7 join walk 48 at Map 1. At the end of walk 48 rejoin walk 47 at Map 8

<u>Walk 48 and 52</u> Start walk 48 and at Map 6 join walk 52 at Map 1. Leave walk 52 at Map 1 and rejoin walk 48 at Map 6 to complete walk 48 . (4 hours)

<u>Walk 51 and 52 :</u> Start walk 51 and at Map 5 join walk 52 at Map 1 and complete walk 52 (4 hours)

<u>Walk 53 and 55:</u> Do walk 53 then join walk 55 between map 1 and 2 in Benalauria and complete walk 55 (3 hours)

<u>Walk 55 and 54</u> Start walk 55 and at Map 4 join walk 54 at the start on the main road . Complete walk 54 and rejoin walk 55 at Map 4. (5 hours)

<u>Walk 54 and 42:</u> Start walk 54 and at Map 3 join walk 42; between map 3 and 4 turning right . At Map 3 on walk 42

after 100 metres rejoin walk 54 at Map 4 and complete walk 54 (5 hours)

Walk 55 and 56: These walks start at the same place so a figure of 8 walk is possible.

Walk 59 and 60: These walks start at the same place so a figure of 8 walk is possible .

iv. RIGHTS OF WAY

As in most countries there is an issue as to whether public rights of way exist or whether the land owner can prohibit access. This area is no exception, and perhaps is a prime example in Spain where there is poor or non-existent documentation on ownership and rights of way, so there are several grey areas. In the past this has not mattered, but in this age of increased mobility, leisure time and access to the countryside, combined with more proprietarial owners, rights of way have become contentious. In this area there are theoretically undisputed historical public rights of way, known as cañadas (up to 75 metres wide) and veredas (15 metres wide): examples in this book are La Cañada real de Benarraba (walk 32)   and Vereda del Pescadero (walk 31) . These were drovers' routes. Another category is the Via Pecuaria, another form of agricultural right of way, which is recorded very inaccurately on documents held in townhalls called 'Croquis de las Vias Pecuarias del Termino Municipal de ....   For example Gaucin`s dates from 1968.

Another important feature is the publicly owned land around Gaucin and Jimena known as Monte Publico. Examples include the lower slopes of the Hacho mountain and the forested land north of the village to the west of the main Ronda road. This land is freely accessible to the public and is found on walks 33 and 34 . The only drawback is that on very rare occasions it could be closed off as a fire risk or for tree-felling or other work. An example is in walk 36 , where an exit gate has in recent years been padlocked during the chestnut season to stop unauthorised chestnut picking.

Signposted walks

In the past 20 years Spain at local and national level has introduced the European system of path marking . This consists of:

1: red and white markers for long distance paths (Gran recorridos) (GR) examples found here are the GR 141 Gran Senda de la Serranía de Ronda , (eg walk 39) the GR 249 Gran Senda de Malaga (eg walk 55) and the GR 7 the Tarifa to Athens path which features in walks 22 and 25 .

2: yellow and white markers for medum distance paths (pequenos recorridos) (PR) generally linking villages together. You will see these frequently on these walks .

3: green and white markers for local paths (senda local) (SL) .Created and marked up by town halls and are paths that start and finish in a particular village .

Lastly there are local paths, not necessarily recorded in public documents, or marked,   which villagers have used for centuries to reach their fincas (smallholdings), and which pass through other people's land. These are probably the most contentious; many are regarded by the authorities as public rights of way for agricultural workers, but in recent times they have begun to be used for leisure activities like walking and riding, and at the same time the owners of the land they pass through, often new owners not previously connected with the countryside, are demanding, and attempting to enforce, their privacy.

However, there are local paths that are definitely public and can be found in the 1968 document mentioned above and the equivallents in all the vilages in this area.

Notwithstanding all the above, in nearly 40 years of walking in this area I have only been challenged as a potential trespasser on about 4 occasions, and on none of the routes in this book .

v. GENERAL INFORMATION ABOUT WALKING

The best time of year to visit the area is in Spring and Autumn when the climate is most suitable for walking; however the winters can be warm with good visibility – you just need to be aware of the rains that can come between November and April and the heat that is ever present in July and August. It is possible to walk all year round – it is just necessary to choose the appropriate hour according to the season.

In this area trees include cork oaks, Holm oaks, chestnuts, pines, poplars, carobs, almonds, olives and figs. Due to the predominance of evergreen species even in winter the impression is always one of abundant greenery.

Within the woodland is abundant undergrowth, with gorse, broom, heathers and lavender, and of course many perennial wild flowers such as the narcissus in winter and the orchids and peonies in spring. The quieter walker may be lucky and see fox, mongoose, badger and wild boar - the latter evident through its excavating activities. Birdlife is ever present and ranges from the Griffon vultures and other raptors to the numerous migratory birds which pass through the Genal and Guadiaro valleys in March and September. Cattle, sheep, pigs and goats are prevalent in the area; if you are lucky you may see the Ibex Iberico, a cross between a deer and goat which is common in the mountains around. Deer are also found in the area.

Of course, the main attraction of walking in this area is the opportunity to enjoy the marvellous views in all directions. On the southern horizon, beyond the hills between the Valleys of the Genal and the Guadiaro Rivers, looms the Rock of Gibraltar with the Rif mountains of Africa behind it. To the East lies the wooded valley of the Genal, with its scattered white villages framed by the red- rocked Sierra Bermeja and the rugged peaks of the Crestellina range. To the north are the bare peaks of the Sierra de las Nieves, and to the west, from the top of the Hacho mountain, one can see the valley of the Guadiaro with open fields and La Brutrera , a deep limestone gorge eroded by the river Guadiaro and inhabited by the eponymous vulture with the Sierra de Libar behind the village of Cortes. At the southern end the valley of the Hozgarganta forms one of the boundaries of the Natural Park of the Alcornocales, one of the largest wild areas of Europe

Finally, I offer the usual but vital advice. I am sure that all walking enthusiasts will be aware that the weather can change rapidly in this part of Spain on the border between the Mediterranean and Atlantic climates. Make sure you allow enough daylight for your walk. Take something to drink and, for the longer walks, something to eat. It is imperative to have comfortable footwear with well-gripping soles, and advisable to wear long trousers as the paths are sometimes a little overgrown and gorse is prevalent.

In the warmer seasons sun cream is recommended. Please respect the environment, remember to close all gates which you have had to open. Do not disturb the farm animals you may come across especially if you are accompanied by dogs; these must always be on a lead.

Please be aware that new gates and fences may appear which do not feature in the descriptions; I would be most grateful to hear about these, and also to receive any comments and suggested alterations in English or Spanish for future editions of this guide book: please send to the email address below.

robertpatrickelvin@gmail.com

vi. MORE INFORMATION ABOUT WALKING IN GAUCIN AND OTHER ACTIVITIES

Gaucín Walking club

The author organises walks in the area free of charge, on two week days every week from September to June, ranging from 2 to 7 hours. You can contact him for further details: robertpatrickelvin@gmail.com

Guides and Walking Tours

Jorrian van der Schaaf is a local guide who can arrange all ranges of walk, from a couple of hours at 40 Euro to a full-package walking holiday of a week of walking from village to village for 650 Euro a person. He speaks Dutch, English,

German and Spanish. See www.walkingwildandalucia.com
or call him on   +34 658 612 989.

Further walks

The author has made descriptions of a number of walks on
separate leaflets which he sells for 1 Euro. Contact him on
robertpatrickelvin@gmail.com

vii. MORE BOOKS ON WALKING

Patrick Elvins Amazon publication Walks around Gaucin
contains 21 walks based on the village of Gaucin. These are
all different from the walks in this book

CEDER Serranía de Ronda, 2005 has edited Senderos
Serranía de Ronda with 30 walks. It has been translated into
English. The maps are good, but the descriptions are
sometimes unreliable.

Editorial La Serranía S.L., 2007 published Valle del Genal,
Guia del excursionísta by Rafael Floris Dominguez with 57
trails for walking and cycling, in Spanish.

Guy Hunter-Watts wrote Walking in Andalucia, Ediciones
Santana S.L. 2010 and also Cicerone publications with walks

in 6 natural parks all over Southern Spain, amongst them two walks near Gaucín and others round Jimena .

viii. ACKNOWLEDGEMENTS

Firstly to my wife Susan who has tirelessly edited every page with her indomitable thoroughness.

Secondly to Matthew Wolfman and Roger Collinson who have contributed GPS tracks for several walks which you can download to your device from wikilocs.

Thirdly to members of the Gaucin walking club who have accompanied me during the research for these walks and have proof tested nearly all of the instructions. I would like to mention in particular Roger Collinson, Annie Mooney, Steven Peacock, Richard McCaie, Phil Wood, Linda Piggot, Brigitte Bianchetti, Matthew Wolfman, Ingrid Knutson, Colin Hayman, Bill and Teresa Tilden, Calum Chace (who also convinced me to renumber all the walks to follow on from my first volume of wallks) . These good friends have painstakingly and independently between them walked every metre of these 40 walks and contributed helpful improvements to the texts .

WALK 22 JIMENA - LAS ASOMADILLAS

Time: 2 hours (7 kilometres)

Difficulty : easy

Terrain: mainly rough paths , some track .

Brief description : This walk has been marked by the Jimena Town hall with white arrows so it should be easy to follow . Essentially a river valley walk with an an element of height gain early on which will give good views of Jimena .

HOW TO GET THERE . From A 405/A369 take the Ubrique road   . Park near the camping site which is a turn back into Jimena at the top of the hill after 2 kilometres.

Downloadable wikiloc track
https://www.wikiloc.com/wikiloc/view.do?id=2081029

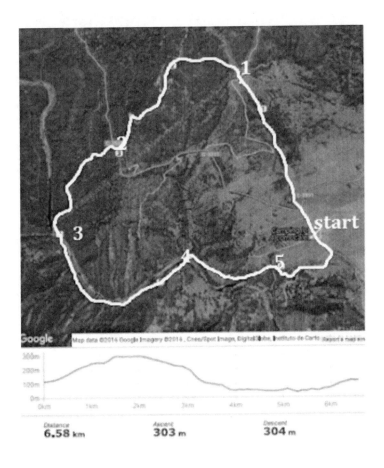

http://gb.mapometer.com/walking/route_4447591.html

Map showing waypoints in directions (white numbers) , disstance in kilometres (small numbers) and an elevation profile

THE WALK   Start the walk at the camping site . Head north
leaving Jimena behind you and cross over at the junction
100 metres up the road .

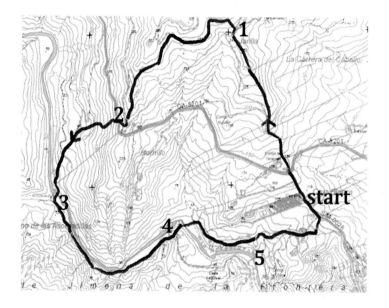

This is the GR 7 long distance footpath which you follow for
the first part of the walk. Head up the hill on this rough
path, cobbled in places .   After 20 minutes you arrive at a
driveable track after passing through a gate . (Map 1)
(36.454026° -5.466711°) Turn right and go a few metres
and take a left turn just before a gate across the track which
will be signposted as the GR 7 . Head up the slope looking
for a white arrow on a post pointing to the left . It is near a
solitary cork tree . Follow the white arrows which will lead
you through pine trees slightly down hill on a track which
eventually arrives at a metal gate. (Map 2) (36.447297°
-5.474403°) Take a small path just before the gate which

heads up past a pedestrian gate towards a rocky outcrop. (enjoy the views from here as shortly you will be descending to the river) When you see a fence ahead and below follow it round to the right and downhill where there is a gate leading to the road below .

Cross the road looking for the path the other side descending into the pine woods. Follow this path for 10 minutes when it joins a forestry track. Turn left and continue down to the river passing through a gate at the bottom of the woods in the process . (Map 3) (36.443085° -5.479721°) Cross the river on concrete stepping stones and turn left onto the path which continues downstream on the right hand side of the river Hozgarganta. This path does not stray far from the river bank, but at one stage it veers sharply to the right up the rocks to traverse this rocky outcrop. There are markings at this point. A little further on the path emerges onto a flat area with farm buildings ahead and caged dogs on the right . (Map 4) (36.440929° -5.470161°)

At this point veer left towards the river, pass through a wire and post gate and slightly to the right there is a set of concrete stepping stones similar to the ones you crossed earlier. The path enters the trees and veers right , cobbled in places.   After a gate it passes to the left of a finca, becomes a track and starts to rise to meet a track coming up from the river. (Map 5) (36.440674° -5.463028°) Turn left and climb back up to the street and turn left to reach the campsite which you will have noticed to your left on your ascent from the river.

WALK 23 - SAN PABLO - ABOVE THE GUADIARO

Time : 2.5 hours (7.5 kilometres)

Difficulty : moderate

Terrain : tracks and some very rough paths . One overgrown section but avoidable . See text

BRIEF DESCRIPTION: a varied walk through cork woods with great views later in the walk. One overgrown section which can be avoided

HOW TO GET THERE   On the A369 Gaucin to Jimena road in San Pablo opposite the Restaurante Las Cachollas take a tarmaced track heading through orange groves . Drive 3 Kilometres down , and park just before it arrives at gates . The last part is not tarmacked . If you dont wish to drive on this rather rough   non tarmaced section park outside the entrance gates to a house called EL Diplomatico Feo , an excellent B and B and walk the rest of the way. It is 1.2 Kilometres to this point from the main road and   will add 50 minutes to your timings .

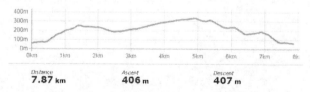

Distance	Ascent	Descent
7.87 km	**406** m	**407** m

Wikilocs reference courtesy Matthew Wolfman

https://es.wikiloc.com/wikiloc/view.do?id=16957130

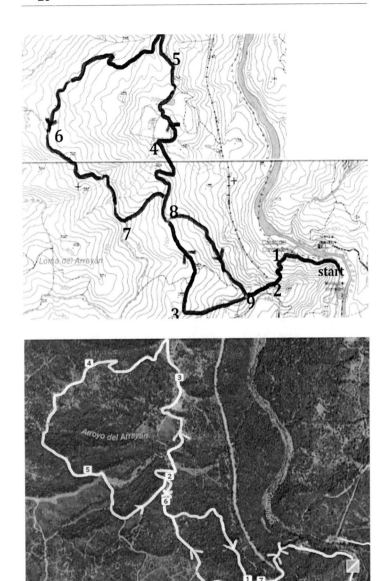

http://gb.mapometer.com/walking/route_4508637.html

THE WALK Pass through the gates a few metres beyond where you have parked the car. There is a sign in 2017 warning of construction work . You will pass clear of any work which is going on in the abandoned village. In five minutes you willl arrive at the abandoned village formerly workers cottages for the power station on the other side of the river. It is currently being restored as holiday cottages.

As you arrive pass one house on your left above you and then veer left leaving the main track between the second house above you and the top house of a row going down towards the river . Map 1) (36.495203° -5.407785°) Look for a flat metal bridge crossing a ditch and follow the path up the slope the other side . The path enters woods by a cork tree and then shortly passes through a gate . Continue climbing into the woods for 100 metres where the path splits; veer left up the slope (cairn here) and after 5 minutes you will see the railway as it enters a tunnel to your right . Keep going straight up the path which veers sharply right after 60 metres from the tunnel and soon you will see a fence to your left and ahead . (Map 2) (36.493418° -5.408962°) Look for a gate to your left. Pass through and then continue to follow this fence up the ridge . Once through the gate it is easier to skirt left up and round the large rock in front of you and then rejoin the fence . After 150 metres (4 minutes) there is another metal gate in the fence . Pass through and after a few metres veer left to continue up the ridge on a wide but rough indistinct path . After about 5 minutes of climbing you arrive at a track . (Map 3) (36.493734° -5.414555°) Turn right and follow this track for 1 kilometre (15 minutes) . At this point you need to look for a rough track turning right . (Map 4) (36.500482° -5.416392°) You should be able to see a finca ahead in a cleared flat area . The track is 100 metres before the entrance gate to this finca. Go 100 metres down this track and there is a clearing . Go slightly left through a gap in the bushes to find a metal gate .

Pass through the gate and plunge down to a stream . Cross over and folllow a fence to your left through woods until you reach a track . Turn left and soon you will meet a track emerging from the aforementioned finca on your left. Turn right and only a few metres after passing a second track off to the left , then by a pond on your left, veer sharp right up the slope to shortly pass a small lake on your right.. 200 metres past the lake (Map 5) (36.505298° -5.416016°) take the left fork and follow this track for about 20 minutes as it gently climbs to about 300 metres. At this point take a left fork entering thicker woods , (cairn here) the track very soon does a sharp right turn as it meets a fence. As soon as you have turned this corner look for a small path up to your left heading up alongside the fence . (Map 6) (36.501581° -5.424762°) Follow this for 25 metres where there is a gate. Pass through and follow this pretty path heading towards the ridge ahead in a southerly direction before crossing the ridge where there is a small clearing (500 metres from the gate) with a large rock from which there are great views down the valley and beginning to descend. 5 minutes from the large rock (350 metres) turn left off the main track (Map 7) (36.496773° -5.419297°) down a rough path which descends straight down the hill for 5 minutes to meet the track you were on earlier . (It is a bit rough where the path meets the track as a bulldozer has been at work) . Turn right on to the track you were on earlier . Careful navigation is needed here to ensure you dont miss the next turning which is 200 metres along the track . (Map 8) (36.496815° -5.416204°) (If you are of a cautious nature and unconfident about finding your way through thick woods you may prefer to continue along the track and retrace your steps along the first part of the walk as the next section is over grown in places and has the potential for getting you lost!!) A couple of cairns mark the turn off to the left which initially has been cleared by a bulldozer but essentially is a foot path heading straight down the hillside ignoring all turnings for 300 metres (5 minutes) . At this point you should veer right, (a cairn should indicate this), and then you will roughly follow the contour line for the next section which can be overgrown in places . Cairns have been placed at various points to help guide you . At one point you will pass through a wire and post gate and then meet a more overgrown section before the path improves and rises up to a ridge where you will rejoin the route you started on earlier . As you reach the ridge there is a fence ahead and slightly to the right is the gate you passed through earlier . (Map 9) (36.492371° -5.411550°) Once through the gate turn left and follow the fence down until you reach the lower gate . Just before there is a primitive stile apparently designed for goats to climb ! You can use this to cross the fence . The path the other side drops down to the abandoned village passing by the railway line on the way .

WALK 24 - JIMENA -TO THE LOMO DEL CAÑUELO

Time : 2 hours 15 minutes (7.5 Kilometres)

Difficulty: moderate

Terrain: some road rough tracks and rough paths

Brief description: a fine walk with good views over Jimena , a walk back down a valley passing a ruined mill before reaching the Hozgarganta on the final part. Navigation can be tricky .

HOW TO GET THERE . Drive into Jimena from the A405 and after passing over two roundabouts, take the first left (immediately after the Bar-Restaurante Cuenca on the right). This is the Calle Pasada de Alcala. Drive down this road which curves round the side of Jimena before crossing the Rio Hozgarganta.   Park where you can on the other side. Round the next corner there is space on the left off the road

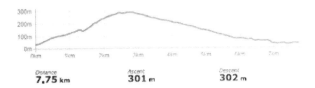

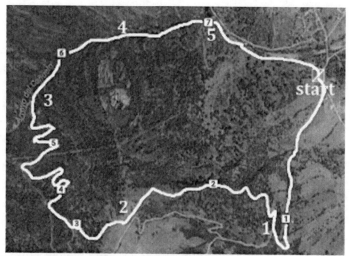

http://gb.mapometer.com/walking/route_4449001.html

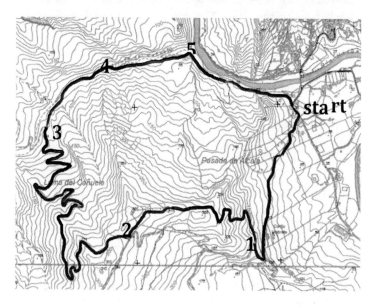

THE WALK. Continue along this road which starts to climb the hill, meandering a little. You can cut the corners. After 20 minutes you will pass Finca Las Limas on the left just as you take a hairpin bend to the right and 100 metres further up you leave the road as it takes a left hairpin bend. (MAP 1) (36.417914° -5.455848°) Take a rough track to the right which passes through a metal gate and drops down to a ruin. At the ruin go sharp left up a very rough track. The track veers left and climbs straight up the hill . Then bear right into the trees and soon there will be a fence on the right . The track bears left away from the fence before bearing right again and rejoining the fence . You have more or less reached the top of the hill so make sure you look back to enjoy the view. The track follows the line of the fence and later a wall along the top of the hill before emerging into more open countryside and you should see the road you left earlier climbing the hill to your left . The track passes through a wire and post gate then veers left towards the road and as you reach the road just keep to the right hand side for a few metres and look for another track heading off the road to the right and down the slope. (MAP 2) (36.418166° -5.465646°)

You will follow this track which zigzags frequently as it descends to the valley floor for three kilometres. There are opportunities to cut the corners. As you approach the valley floor, and at the last of the left hand hairpin bends look for a path off to the right marked by a cairn which will then run parallel to the Cañuelo stream on the left . (MAP 3) (36.424564° -5.472280°) (If you reach a concrete crossing over the stream on the track you have come too far and you should retrace your steps   ) After turning off at the cairn, stay along this side of the river for 100m or so, until it then crosses the stream. Pick up the path on the other side and turn right, now on the left bank.

After just 100m, you cross back over the river, back to the right bank.

Then after 200m you will see a massive boulder on the opposite bank, sitting on top of an old stone wall. At about the same time, on your side of the river, the way becomes considerably more rocky with impassable boulders blocking the way ahead, so cross the stream again here at the easiest point, picking up the trail on the opposite bank and continuing to your right, downstream.

 You pass by some large rocks and after 100 metres you will reach the ruins of the Molino San Francisco. (MAP 4) (36.428088° -5.467034°) After the mill the path drops down to the stream, crosses rather indistinctly and continues the other side for about 20 minutes until it reaches a wire and post gate the other side of which is the Rio Hozgarganta. (MAP 5) (36.428915° -5.461073°) Turn immediately right and follow this well used path along the river bank keeping the fence to your right to the road where you left your car .

WALK 25- JIMENA - CAÑUELO AND THE LOMO DE CADIZ

Time: 3 hours (8.8 Kilometres)

Difficulty: medium due to climb

Terrain : mainly small rough paths

Brief description: A tricky route to navigate (it is recommended to use the wikilocs track) but well rewarded with great views back to Jimena and up the Hozgarganta . A ruined mill and attractive stream on the way up. (For Waymark points 4 -9 I have not put Lat and Long positions because they are not accrate enouogh to be of use)

HOW TO GET THERE   Arrive in Jimena on A405 . Take CA 3331   to Ubrique which skirts round the east and below Jimena. Turn left at the top of the rise and park near the Camping Alcornocales. Walk 100 metres further into town from the Camping and there is a rough track off to the right with an information board .   (If you want to keep the walk to 2 hours you can drive to the bottom of the track and save 30 minutes, but the track is rather rough)

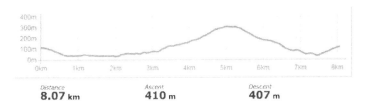

https://www.wikiloc.com/wikiloc/view.do?id=17176413
wikilocs track courtesy Matthew Wolfman

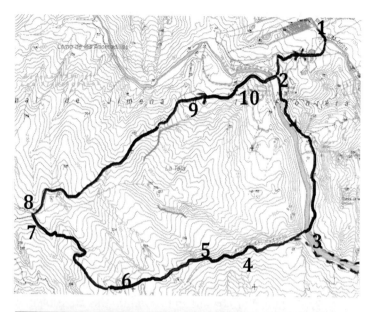

http://gb.mapometer.com/walking/route_4447401.html
Map showing distances in kilometres/ link to mapometer

Start of the walk. (Map 1) (36.441746° -5.458815°)

Walk down this track passing a house on the right ignoring
one turn off to the left and then one to the right ; You
should head down hill towards the rio Hozgarganta .

Just before the river take a small path to the left Into
oleander bushes (Map 2) (36.439495° -5.463680°)
marked by a small post with a white arrow and follow the
river down stream for about a kilometre (20 minutes) After
10 minutes the path becomes a track.

Look on the right and when a wall like construction appears
(actually a channel to take water to a disused bomb
factory, look for a small path dropping down just before the
wall heading for the river. (Map 3) (36.429099°
-5.459785°) (If there has been heavy rain this crossing may
not possible in which case continue to the road , cross the
bridge and return along the opposite bank along a well used
path. Move to the asterisk in the directions.)

 Cross over the river at this point using the remains of the
dam and head into bushes on the other side. You need to
go about 50 metres to find a path coming in from the left
along a fence. * This is the path you have followed if you
crossed via the bridge. Turn right and look for a wire and
post gate about 50 metres further on .

 Pass through and immediately climb a rocky path and
follow for about 20 minutes as it runs above and parallel to
a stream called the Cañuelo. There are frequent small paths
off to the left up the slope. Make sure you keep on the
main path being aware of the stream below and to your
right .

Eventually it drops down to the stream and crosses over through bushes . This is not obvious but once you are across make sure you locate the path as it climbs up the other side heading towards a ruined mill on the left. (Map 4)

Continue up beyond the mill making sure you take a left fork in the path 30 metres beyond the mill . You are now walking parallel to the stream, but after only 100 metres you cross back over to locate a path in the rocks initially climbing up the rocks but soon settling down to follow the stream.

 You now walk on the left hand side for a further 300 metres , looking for yet another crossing. (Map 5) Again this is not particularly obvious (there are scrubby oleander bushes at this point , but once across you now head into the woods up a path going uphill marked by an occasional cairn. The direction here is north west. At first the path appears to go more north east but it does veer round to the left heading up to a ridge.

The path crosses over this ridge and then reaches a flat rocky area with a trickle of a stream coming down this gully. Cross over and head up the next ridge; there should be more cairns to help and when you cross over this next ridge you should look out for a pylon and a stand of eucalyptus trees . This is your direction but the path is hard to follow as it splits in several places.   However make sure you leave the pylon close to your left and then after 100 metres you will reach a track in the eucalyptus. (Map 6)

   Cross over the track, go up a bank and leave a ruined building to your right and enter a clearing. Cross over the clearing heading to another small ruin. Pass to the left of this ruin , cross a gully and head slightly right up the hill on a faint path marked by cairns. Your direction is more north. You pass through two very small grassy clearings and then the path starts zigzagging and climbs more steeply and generally edges to the left. When the path levels out and you have gone about 200 metres look out for a right turn marked by a cairn (Map 7) . Turn right up a very steep and rough path a bit overgrown and climb 50 metres to reach a fence with a wire and post gate . (Map 8)

On the other side of the gate turn right along a clearer path which you follow down hill for 20 minutes until it reaches an open area with the river Hozgarganta down to the left and craggy cliffs up to the right . At the far end the path passes through some trees, enters another open area, passes over a shoulder , through more trees and descends down another grassy open area strewn with stones and rocks. The river is ahead and below.

Below you about 100 metres ahead there are the remains of a stone wall running at 90 degrees to your direction. (Map 9) At this point you head to the right, keeping the wall on your left, into trees looking for a fence, which is across a rocky gully about 100 metres into the trees on the same contour line and then a gate in the fence. This gate is near a wet muddy area . Pass through the gate and continue on the contour line for 5 minutes arriving at a partially built cottage . Leave the cottage to your left and join a faint track descending towards a well used track coming from a farm to the left. Turn right and follow to the river where it crosses on a ford. You meet the track down which you came earlier. (Map 10) Just retrace your steps up the hill.

WALK 26 - SAN PABLO TO EL CERRO DEL BUHO

Time : 2 hours 7 Kilometres

Difficulty : Easy

Terrain : Mainly tracks, one rough path

Brief description: A picturesque walk with relatively little climbing and is easy to follow. Views of San Pablo and the Guadiaro river . (Buho is spanish for owl)

HOW TO GET THERE

From Jimena take the A405 direction Gaucin, Pass a petrol station on your left then after a couple of bends take a track to the left by an aqueduct which passes over the road.

From Gaucin take A 405 direction Jimena . When you reach San Pablo pass one Venta on the right by the bridge over the Guadiaro then after a second Venta on the left and a car garage, take a track on the right by an aqueduct passing over the road

After 100 metres up the track take a right fork; this is known as Calle Acueducto . Continue until you reach the railway and park here.

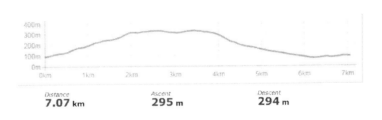

Distance
7.07 km

Ascent
295 m

Descent
294 m

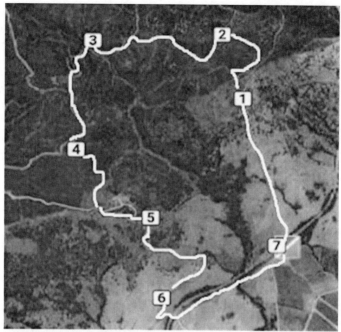

http://gb.mapometer.com/walking/route_4447151.html
Map showing route with kilometre markers / link to
mapometer

THE WALK . Map (1)   36.480244° -5.414138°)
Cross over the railway and head uphill on a concrete track
which soon turns to gravel. Pass a farm on your left then
pass through a large metal gate with various farm animals
appearing on your right. (Map 2) (36.488642°
-5.417477°) The track gets steeper and climbs to a
padlocked gate . Pass through a pedestrian gate a few
metres to the left or climb the ladder stile. Continue for 170
metres; about 3 minutes, passing one rough track to the
left then looking for a second rough track to the left. (Map
3) (36.492099° -5.415149°) Take this which narrows to a
path, climbing the hillside and becoming a rough track after

passing over an open grassy patch . Another rough track joins from the right, but continue up until you reach a more substantial track where you turn left. (Map 4) (36.492904° -5.418334°)

Follow the contour line on this track passing a container converted to farm use, and then cross a small stream. The track splits after this . Take either one as they rejoin after 100 metres. The track climbs to meet a track coming down the hill. (Map 5) (36.489495° -5.428976°)

Turn left and follow for 500 metres / 8 minutes noting one path to the left and then looking for a second path to the left at the 500 metre point. (Map 6) (36.485798° -5.429563°) This path winds down the hill above farm buikdings before passing a water tank on the right and then arriving at a track. (Map 7) (36.482415° -5.427974°)

Turn left , pass through a gate and follow this track down hill as it heads towards the railway and San Pablo. When you arrive at a gate (probably padlocked) climb through the small door in the right hand gate and head for the railway line. (Map 8) (36.475785° -5.422112°) Cross over then take a faint track to the left running up the side of the railway into the trees and then emerging near where you have parked your car.

WALK 27- COLMENAR – A WALK IN THE WOODS

Time: 2 hours (6.6 Kilometres)
Difficulty: easy
Terrain: mainly track , 2 sections on paths

Brief description: a gentle walk mainly through woodland
above Colmenar in the Alcornocales Natural Park.   Some
tricky navigation in the woods whilst on the first path.

HOW TO GET THERE
take the MA512 Gaucin to Colmenar road 2 K from Gaucin
in A405 direction Algeciras and continue until you reach the
village of Colmenar having crossed the Rio Guadiaro . Drive
into the village; park just before the level crossing.

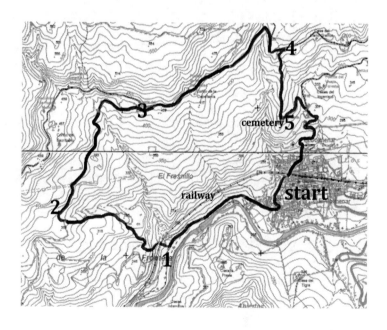

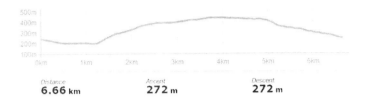

http://gb.mapometer.com/walking/route_4455648.html

Downloadable wikiloc track courtesy Roger Collinson

http://www.wikiloc.com/wikiloc/view.do?id=17386376

THE WALK Walk towards the level crossing and just before there is a sign La Presa on the left. Take this concrete road and follow it until it reaches a junction of several streets. Turn right to follow Calle de la Presa which immediately becomes a gravel track and leaves the village to head towards the river which will appear on your left after 10 minutes. Ignore any turnings to the left . You will notice a pedestrian bridge across the river above the dam (la Presa) and then a parking area on the left and a shabby finca on the right with a prominent blue tarpaulin. Continue 100 metres crossing a rough concrete bridge then 50 metres after that take a small path to the right up the slope which leads to the railway line. (MAP 1) (36.535762° -5.398138°)Cross the railway, go through a wire and post gate then take a path up the hill ignoring one path immediately on the left . Your path also turns left, passes through an open grassy area, climbs a little more and meets a rough track. Turn right here and soon you will pass a house to the right. The track bends to the left and then to the right.   On this right bend, take a path to the left which passes by a cork tree and then zigzags up through trees before widening and straightening on a more level part of the hillside. It then climbs again and within 50 metres look for a path off to the right by a tree whose trunk base has grown over a rock. Go up this path taking care to take a left fork up a steep rocky slope after 50 metres. This path is a bit indistinct and rocky to start with but soon develops into an easy to follow clear path. After a few minutes you will emerge on to a wide rough track . (MAP 2) (36.537382° -5.406765°)

Turn right and follow passing one house on the right, then a cattle grid, then two houses on the left before joining a

better quality track. (MAP 3) (36.544535° -5.399197°)
Turn right and you will soon have a great view down to
Colmenar . The track follows the contour until it drops
down slightly, turns right and then meets a narrow tarmac
road

Turn right, and after 50 metres there is a left hand bend ; 50
metres after the bend there is a rough path off to the right
(MAP 4) (36.548044° -5.389088°) doubling back briefly
before bearing left down the ridge amongst eucalyptus and
fir trees. After 10 minutes a building appears below and you
will emerge onto a car park alongside the village cemetery,
a tranquil place.   (MAP 5) (36.543681° -5.388723°)

Leave the cemetery via the road which after 5 minutes joins
the road you were briefly on earlier and turning right , this
road will lead you back to the village. Notice on the left
signs for the arboretum, worth a detour. A rough path
allows you to cut corners . At the first houses take a side
street called Calle del Semillero which will lead you straight
down.   When you reach the main street turn right then
immediately left to reach the level crossing and your car the
other side .

Things of interest in and around Colmenar

Arboretum

the Bruitrera Gorge Up the GR 141

Canis restaurant

A drive through the Alcornocales to Cortes

WALK 28- GAUCIN - DOWN TO THE GUADIARO

Time; 2 hours (6 Kilometres)
Difficulty : moderate (rocky climb)
Terrain: track then rough paths

Brief description: an exciting walk that takes you down to
the banks of the rio Guadiaro , just north of Colmenar
(Estacion de Gaucin) . The views are of the Guadiaro
looking north and south.

HOW TO GET THERE

Take the MA512 Gaucin to Colmenar road 2 K from Gaucin
oin A405 direction Algeciras and continue until just after
Kilometre 8 marker post . There is a sharp left hand bend
with a track leading off to the right . Park here .

THE WALK

Head down this track for just over one kilometre (15 to 20
minutes) passing several fincas.

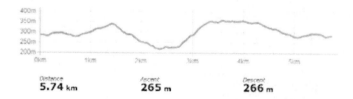

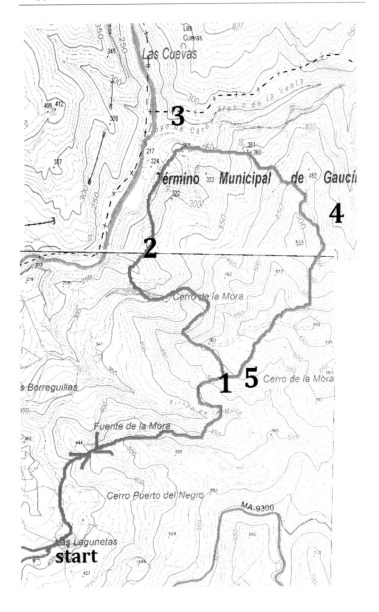

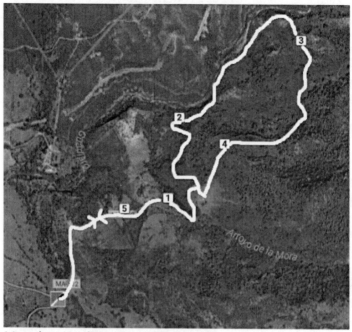

Map showing distances in kilometres

http://gb.mapometer.com/walking/route_4449235.html

After a kilometre (15 -20 minutes) pass through a gate and
continue round a small hill where there is a goat farm up
ahead . (MAP 1) (36.537384° -5.369513°) As the track
turns up to the farm leave the track by going off to the left
following the fence which has been on your left as you came
up the track. Just on the corner there is a path descending
through the fence via a wire and post gate (probably open
) . There is a tree with blue paint marks on its trunk . Go
through the gate and follow this path down until it reaches a
grassy plateau. (MAP 2) (36.538247° -5.374201°)

Turn sharp right here and continue down towards the river below and to your left. Eventually the path reaches the level of the river and a little further up arrivies at an open grassy area. (MAP 3) (36.543435° -5.367231°) There is a faint path off to the left which passes an orange tree , but you need to veer right past an agave in a gap in the bushes and then left to a rough path going up the side of a ridge running up from the river to the right.

Follow this rough path as it keeps to the right of the ridge and climbs to a small grassy plateau, where there is a ruin in the bushes. Continue upwards crossing the centre of this gully and head right up the rough path into the trees. After 5 minutes you will arrive at a more well worn path coming along the contour line. (MAP 4) (36.541272° -5.363648°)

Turn right here and follow it as it continues along the contour line above some cliffs before emerging on to a flatter area littered with broom bushes and with the goat farm you saw earlier ahead . As you approach a fence look for the gate at the right hand edge. (MAP 5) (36.536903° -5.369080°) Pass through and head for the track you came up on earlier in the walk. Turn right on to the track and retrace your steps .

WALK 29- GAUCIN - CERRO LAS MARAVILLAS

Time: 2 hours (6.7 kilometres)

Difficulty: medium

Terrain. About half on track and half on a rough indistinct
path through woods.

Brief description: This walk takes you up the Cerro Las
Maravillas to a height of 646 metres and offers great views
up and down the Guadiaro valley and across to La Herriza.
The walk is a mixture af a good track and a very rough and
indistinct path. (You can extend the walk by parking nearer
the road and walking down the track to the start)

HOW TO GET THERE

take the MA512 Gaucin to Colmenar road 2 K from Gaucin
on A405 direction Algeciras and continue until just after you
pass a walled gated entrance to La Herriza country hotel .
1 kilometre further on there is a track going sharply to the
left with a stop sign facing down the track .

Drive down this track (the Cañada Real de Benarraba) and
after about 500 metres pass a low white building (place to
park if you want to extend the walk) on your right and later
pass through a wire and post gate (probably open) . After
a further 500 metres go through an open metal gate over a
cattle grid into a eucalyptus grove .   Park here.

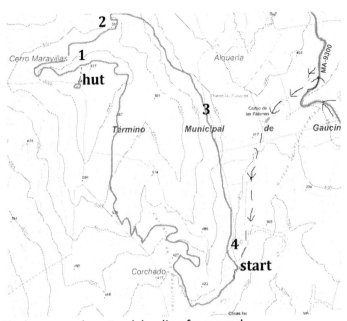

Black arrows show track leading from road

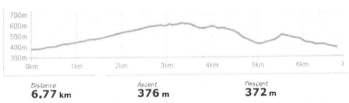

Distance	Ascent	Descent
6.77 km	**376** m	**372** m

If you wish to download the track this is the wikilocs link
(courtesy of Matthew Wolfman)

https://www.wikiloc.com/wikiloc/view.do?id=15861581

THE WALK . There are three tracks leading from here. 30 metres from the gate take the first right fork and the uppermost of the three tracks with a chain across.

After two hundred metres pass through a wire and post gate and continue up the hill: the track starts zig zagging - you can cut the corners but you may prefer the gentle gradient of the main track . At one point it crosses a concrete ford and after a further zigzag you go through a wooden gate. The terrain becomes more open and has been cleaned up in the past couple of years . Soon you enter a pine wood and the track makes a sharp turn to the left . (in 2016 major clearance of the pine trees is taking place and the track is very churned up by machinery.)

 The track veers sharp left and then after a few hundred metres starts descending - you pass a sign in the trees saying Tramo VI and V and there is a small white building in the trees up to your left . (Map 1) (36.521850° -5.392582°) (For great views it is worth the short climb up to the building . You can return to the track by following the fence down to your right) As the track approaches a fence it then hairpins to the right and after 500 metres just after the next sharp bend to the left look for a large tree with a half rotten remains of a branch just by the track with a cairn at the foot of the trunk. (Map 2) (36.524753° -5.389681°) 50 metres down to the right look for three cork trees in a line close to each other . Descend to these trees and turn right here and pass to the right of a gnarled cork to follow a faint path . After 50 metres take a left fork which descends slightly before following the contour line. At a gnarled cork oak there is a cairn marking a faintish path following the contour line. Below you on the left there is another metal sign saying Tramo V/VI. At this point the path goes slightly right and here it is a question of spotting cairns to guide you down the slope to join what becomes a more distinct path.

If you are correct you will shortly pass a fallen down cork oak with its branches across the path.

The path descends gently through rocks and trees   The path is indistinct in places in particular when it crosses gullies but you should notice a sawn off tree trunk by the path. You will notice the hotel La Herriza across the fields and soon after this the path crosses a gully and rises a little .

After a further 500 metres you will see another Tramo VI/VII sign in the trees above you on the right and soon the track enters more open flatter ground.

After 5 or so minutes notice a metal posted fence running parallel about 50 metres below. Between the path and the fence therei are thick bushes so you should continue along the path to the right of the bushes passing a rock with a small rock on top. As the bushes give way to open ground start descending towards the fence . There will be a streambed bed here. (Map 3) (36.518045° -5.382346°) Once you reach the fence veer right to walk parallel to this fence on your left. You will see a large villa on your left and then you will reach a fence ahead coming down the hill side . About 30 metres up from the corner where it meets the fence you have been following pass through a gate (Map4) (36.511434° -5.380976°) which will probably be open and then descend slightly left down through the eucalyptus trees to the track on which you started your walk .

Rejoin your car or walk back up the track if you have parked your car further up.

WALK 30 - GAUCIN – PUERTO DEL NEGRO AND THE ALQUERIA PATH

Time: 2 hours 30 minutes (8 Kilometres) (3 hours if you walk out from Gaucin)

Difficulty: easy

Terrain: open fields and woods , rough paths and rough tracks .

Brief description: a relatively gentle walk with great views to Colmenar and the Guadiaro valley as well as diverse terrain including woodland , mountainside and open fields.

HOW TO GET THERE
 Drive out from Gaucin on A405 direction Algeciras for 1.5 Kilometres . After passing Breñaverde venta and the Gaucin water supply both on the left, on a left hand bend there is a path heading off the road to the right: just beyond there is a place to park at the start of a track on the left.

See below for track on wikilocs (courtesy Matthew Wolfman) (starts from village of Gaucin)

http://www.wikiloc.com/wikiloc/view.do?id=15805379

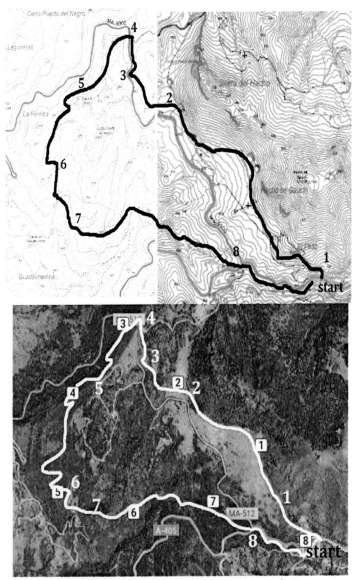

Map with distances in kilometres and map numbers
http://gb.mapometer.com/walking/route_4449057.html

Distance	Ascent	Descent
8.09 km	**377** m	**377** m

THE WALK

Head up the path, passing a ruin and a small spring with a water trough before passing by a quarry on the right above you. You then arrive at a wire and post gate. (MAP1) (36.514821° -5.342358°) Pass through and then as soon as you can, drop down into the open field to avoid the overgrown gorse bushes blocking the rough track. Cross the field keeping parallel to the track above you on the sheep paths before rejoining the track when you can. As the track rounds the corner with the mountainside coming ever closer, be aware of the road down to your left . At a junction of tracks take the left hand track (MAP2) (36.524083° -5.352469°) but almost immediately leave it heading through a copse towards a ridge ahead with the road down on your left . You are aiming for the left hand gap in this ridge. At the foot there is a rough path winding up the side and then passing through the gap. Follow this often narrow and a little overgrown path as it passes down the gully ahead before emerging onto an open area with the road ahead. Head for a gate leading to the road MAP 3) (36.526475° -5.357352°) and turn right to follow the road for 200 metres. Just before a wide track leaving the road to the right, look for a gate up to the left leading into woods. (MAP 4) (36.529234° -5.357722°) Head up into the woods. There is no real path here, just aim for the top, from which you will get great views down to Colmenar and the Guadiaro valley. Continue along the ridge which now gradually descends. When you can see a vineyard on the left leave the ridge on a diagonal path which arrives near a fence, the other side of which is the vineyard. Veer right and a path will lead you along the fence, and then arrives at a track leading into the estate. (MAP 5) (36.525068° -5.361646°) Turn right here and follow the track as it gently descends round the next hill and then zigzags down through woods to the left of the ridge. After passing through a wire and post gate descend further and the track peters out. (MAP 6) (36.517930° -5.366245°) Now look for a rough path marked by cairns off down to the left, passing along a line of cork trees. It starts by going slightly back diagonally before veering to the right through a fence with electric tape (Just step over) to approach a fence . The path then continues down hill parallel to the fence, for 200 metres. It arrives at a path running at right angles. Turn left and immediately pass through a gate.

You will walk this lovely old path uphill for about 2 km. It is known as the Alquería or Los Pilones (meaning either 'pillars' or 'water basins'). It is still partly cobbled and has steps built in to make it firm and prevent it from turning into a streambed in the rainy season, reminders of a past when it was often used.

Your way uphill allows panoramic views to the villages of San Pablo de Buceite, down in the valley and Jimena de la Frontera further away. The path leads to a private property but there is a right of way through the middle. Keep following the good path for 100 metres from the gate where it crosses a gully and bears sharp right. Ten metres further on, take a small path forking left, well -marked with blue paint (don't go straight on downhill).

Shortly after this left fork you arrive at the entrance to a large house with a track on the right. (MAP 7) (36.515834° -5.364121°) There may be alpacas in the fields here. Go slightly left, between two fences, keeping the house on your right. Go through a metal gate, past a goat enclosure on the left and head up towards a square peach coloured electricity box. Follow the path, which goes around the back of the house, past a peach coloured water tank, and through another metal gate to exit the property. Continue along this well marked path passing through one metal gate as it climbs steadily up towards the main road. At one point after crossing a stream bed you veer right then left to pass through a gulch before the path resumes its position on the side of the steep bank above the stream and gorge below.

After passing through a wire and post gate continue upwards and you will approach the main Gaucin to Algeciras road through a more open field. You can't see it at first, but there is a gate at the top right hand corner. (MAP 8) (36.514729° -5.345936°) Exit here and turn left keeping inside the barrier until you reach the junction with the El Colmenar (Estacion de Gaucin) road. Take the Gaucin road to return to your car or the village.

WALK 31 - GAUCIN - EL ABREVEDERO

Time: 2 hours (6 Kilometres)

Difficulty: easy

Terrain: open fields some paths and some tracks

Brief description: a gentle walk, relatively flat a lovely spring walk as there are many flowers. Slightly complicated to navigate due to lack of paths and many gates to locate

HOW TO GET THERE

take the MA512 Gaucin to Colmenar road 2 K from Gaucin oin A405 direction Algeciras and continue until just after you pass a walled gated entrance to La Herriza country hotel . 1 kilometre further on there is a track going sharply to the left with a stop sign facing down the track.

Drive down this track (the Cañada Real de Benarraba) and after about 500 metres pass a low white building and then park on the grass to the right of the track. There is a gate with a stile here.

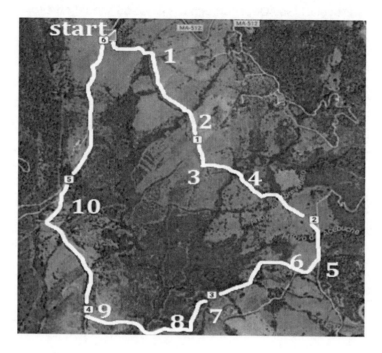

Map showing kilometre markers and map numbers for text

http://gb.mapometer.com/walking/route_4449310.html

wikiloc link courtesy Roger Collinson
https://www.wikiloc.com/wikiloc/view.do?id=16514173

THE WALK

Opposite where you parked your car there is a wire and post gate which is the start of the Vereda del Pescadero . You will follow this ancient right of way for the first part of the walk.

The path is fairly non existent in places and the first part particularly so. Once through the gate you should skirt to the right of the scrubby woods towards a fence on your right.

Then follow the fence towards the corner to your left where there is a wire and post gate leading to an open field . Now follow the fence on your left downhill for about 50 metres looking for a gap. Pass through and then take the upper of two gates about 30 metres up the next field to your right .

 After passing through you now follow the path which may now be more or less non-existent along the bottom edge of this next field. There is a line of wild olives on your right. You are now heading south on the Vereda de los Pescaderos. (MAP 1) (36.517804° -5.375491°) Pass through a wire and post gate at the bottom right hand corner of this field slightly hidden in a gully. (MAP2) (36.514525° -5.373082°)

Cross this gully and then pass along the bottom right hand side of the next field. In the right hand corner go through a gate, bear immediately left and pass through a further gate to cross the next field along the top left hand side. In the corner there are two gates; take the right hand gate which leads to a field where the ground slopes away in front of you. (MAP 3) (36.511310° -5.372123°) Go straight ahead down the slope but heading a bit left towards the bottom left hand corner. You should pass a fallen carob tree in the middle of the field. In the corner there is a gate (see picture below). NB there is also a gate in the fence on the right before you reach the corner .

View towards gate and stile at bottom of this field (line up gate below white building in the distance)

 Pass through and go immediately right following the fence on your right. After a few metres there is a metal ladder/stile which you climb and then turn left to pass through a field keeping the same fence on your left. There are buildings ahead.

Just past the first building there is a gate on the left leading to a track. (MAP 4) (36.509326° -5.368448°) Take this track which bends right after 50 metres and then crosses the arroyo Abrevedero and rises to a wire and post gate. Ignore a track to the left.   Pass through and continue on this track, ignoring a track going obliquely left up to a house after 150 metres. Cross a stream bed and 150 metres later take a track to the right leading to a cottage down the hill. There is a sign here pointing to Los Ranosos (MAP 5) (36.505869° -5.365011°) Before you reach the cottage, look for a gate in the fence to your right, (MAP 6) (36.504987° -5.365996°) pass through and head to the right hand side of the cottage through another gate. Now follow a rough track down the hill heading slightly to the left. Cross a streambed via a wire and post gate and then join a fence on your left which is the boundary of a large villa up to the left. (Los Ranosos) (MAP 7) (36.503631° -5.371011°) Follow this fence ignoring any paths off to the right, at one stage the fence bears left and you will pass some beehives, and then join a track coming down the hill. (MAP 8) (36.501323° -5.373059°) Turn right and drop down crossing a stream at the bottom. Head up the other side , take a left fork 5 minutes from the bottom where the track splits and head towards a line of trees running at right angles to your direction.

In these trees there is a track which you should join, there is gate to the left of where the line of trees finishes . (MAP 9) (36.501456° -5.379292°) Turn right and follow this ancient camino up the hill until it veers right into a eucalyptus grove and joins another track. (MAP 10) (36.509495° -5.380728°)Turn right, cross a cattle grid and pass through a metal gate, and continue on this track until you reach your car.

WALK 32 - GAUCIN – EL PESO AND THE VERANIL VALLEY

Time: 3 hours (9 Kilometres)

Difficulty: hard due to length and height gain . The latter part is very tricky to navigate . I have added white paint markings when the blue markings finish . Only the very intrepid should attempt this walk as it is very overgrown in places and is awaiting strimming by the town hall

Terrain: track, rough paths some overgrown, open fields

Brief description: Although longer than others I have included this walk as it is one of my favourites and would like as many people as possible to enjoy it but with the caveat above . Part of it was created by the mystery blue paint man/woman of Gaucin so I dedicate this walk to him or her whoever he/she may be. The walk covers all types of terrain with unforgettable views. The Ayuntamiento of Gaucin had promised to strim the overgrown section in 2016, but to date not actioned. I have added white paint markers to supplement red and white plastic tape placed for the Ayuntamiento to strim the path from MAP 11 onwards .

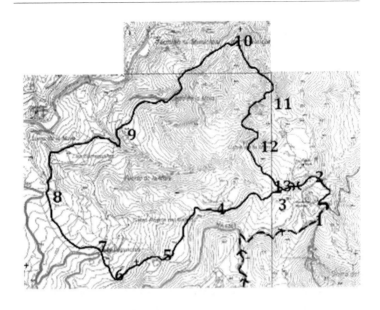

http://gb.mapometer.com/walking/route_4451753.html

Wikiloc map link courtesy Matthew Wolfman

https://www.wikiloc.com/wikiloc/spatialArtifacts.do?
event=setCurrentSpatialArtifact&id=16092601

Distance	Ascent	Descent
9.39 km	**556** m	**560** m

HOW TO GET THERE   Drive from Gaucin on A406 direction
Jimena/Algeciras, and after 2 kilometres take the first right
turn to Colmenar/Estación Gaucin; then after 2 more
kilometres take a large track sharp right as road bends to
the left. Pass over the remains of a cattle grid and drive 1
kilometre until you pass through gates. (Please shut)
Park at the side of the track as it goes round to the right 50
metres further on.

THE WALK On this corner there is a concrete track on the
left passing between two walls with an electric gate. To the
right take the track to the left of a large rock with the house
name "Cortijo El Peso" in green paint and "No Parking;
acceso vehiculos" in peach coloured paint. There are blue
stripes and some red/yellow/white markers on a rock, and a
few metres past the rock you will see a green metal gate
marked with blue stripes. Pass through the gate. You are

now on an old track called "Colada del Camino del Molino al Peso". (MAP 1) (36.531143° -5.348253°) After passing through the gate, walk downhill on the driveable track, ignoring one turning to the left to a pink private house, until you come to a cattle grid. Cross the cattle grid and turn left after two stone pillars on to a small marked path, parallel to a fence. (There is a red and white cross ahead on the main track, indicating you should not continue on the main track). (MAP 2) (36.533260° -5.349720°)

You are now following an old cattle-droving route called "La Cañada Real de Benarraba" that comes from Benarraba, the first village north of Gaucín. After about 50 metres go through a wire and post gate and continue on the main path, keeping to the right (i.e. ignoring any options to the left) until you reach a more open area in the trees by a fence and a streambed.   Here, ignore the small flat path ahead, which is to the right of the fence next to the streambed, and instead bear left and uphill on the wider rocky path and then right . You come out on a small open area in front of a large oak tree. (MAP 3) (36.532044° -5.353892°)The path here is not that obvious at first, but bear left in front of the tree and you will soon spot blue stripes and red/white/yellow stripes on a rock, and then pass an old limestone oven on the right. The path becomes clearer; you cross a streambed and pass through an old wire and post gate.

After ten minutes or so on the rocky path you meet a bigger track; turn left onto the track, which goes uphill, and follow it for a minute ONLY. (MAP 4) (36.530780° -5.359853°)

At the first pylon on the right (marked with plenty of colours
- red/white/yellow paint, blue stripes, and green and white
stripes!) you should leave the main track and take the small
path by the pylon, which leads downhill to an old wire and
post gate. Pass through the gate and keep following the
small path which becomes a rough track bearing left until
you come into a field with a fence ahead. Pass through a
new gate in the middle of the fence (well marked) and cross
the field keeping in the same direction where you meet a
driveable track, with a gate to the left. (MAP 5)
(36.527189°   -5.364403°)

Ignore the track up to the left (do not pass through the
gate) and turn right, walking downhill on the track past a
GR141 marker, until you get to some small metal gates to a
private property ahead. Just before the gates, look for blue
stripes to the right, and follow a rocky path downhill. This
takes you around the house, following the perimeter fence.
Just before the fence finishes at the bottom left hand
corner, look to the right and steeply downhill to find the
continuation of the rocky path. At one point the path seems
to end in an open area by a pylon, but look around to the
left to find it again, marked with blue stripes.   Follow it
downhill to a wire and post gate.

After passing through, continue until you pass a pylon with
red yellow and white stripes.   10 metres further there is a
large wire fence, with a pallet used as a gate, which is the
boundary of La Herriza, a country hotel complex.   Don't go
through but take a rough path to the right leaving the

sewage tank of the hotel on your left. (It can be very wet here and smelly). (MAP 6) (36.525202° -5.370335°)

A few metres further on there is a wire and post gate marked with red white and yellow.   Go through and veer right to follow a faint path downhill.   Entering a scrubby field you should notice the road below and a farmhouse to the right.

Ignore a rough path which heads straight across the field to a gap in the fence but head down the field following the occasional cairn heading just to the right of the road where there is a track which leads to the farmhouse. (MAP 7) (36.527625° -5.371639°)

Pass through the gate, cross over the track and go through the waymarked gate opposite. Veer left following a yellow arrow (waymarks for a new pilgrimage route to Sevilla called La Ruta Jacobea)   which keeps you parallel to the road for 200 metres then turn down the field.

The road does a wide loop while you head down to where you will see the road again and meet another track leaving the road on its next sharp left-hand bend. There is a painted waymark on the rock as you arrive at the track as well as a yellow arrow on a tree. (MAP 8) (36.532366° -5.377217°)

Turn right and follow this track for 1 kilometre passing fincas on your left and right. The track passes a chain between two posts then through a gate before crossing a stream and rising up towards a goat farm. (MAP 9) (36.537716° -5.369489°) As the track bends round to the right towards the farm go straight on keeping close to a fence on your

left, (dont go through the gate on the left in the fence .)
Then pass between a tree and the fence (there may be the
remains of a gate here) to continue on a small path which
enters broom bushes heading north.   You should now be on
a small path heading through broom and gorse slightly
rising but roughly following the contour line along the steep
sides of the cliffs above the river Guadiaro.

1.3 kilometres from the goat farm (about 20 -25 minutes),
CAREFULLY look for a rock just to the left of your path with
blue paint writing, saying Plater. It is easy to miss this rock,
you have gone too far if you arrive at an open area near
the edge of the cliffs below . About 20 metres before this
rock take a path to the right marked by a blue arrow and
climbing steeply after a few metres   (MAP 10) past a tree
with blue arrows (36.543755° -5.359568°) up to a ridge,
then veers right to follow the ridge. There are occasional
blue markings here.   It then keeps to the left of the ridge
as it passes through woods. After 10- 15 minutes of
continuous climbing from the start of the ridge you need to
look out for an oak tree on your right with a large cairn at
its base between the path you are on and the one you will
turn onto. (MAP 11) (36.539526° -5.355792° approx.)
There is a white arrow on the tree pointing to the right . (If
you come to some blue arrows on the main path you have
missed the turn and need to retrace your steps
Turn right at the cairn to follow a very faint and narrow path
which has red and white tape hanging from branches to
show the way (and also for the town hall staff to strim the
path). The path, which is also marked by cairns and in
January 2017 white arrows,   gradually climbs and crosses
two ridges. At these ridges you need to take care not to lose
the path which is overgrown in places . Each time you need

to climb a few metres up the ridge to resume the path and its traverse to the next ridge   before finally arriving at the top of the hill you have been climbing . (MAP 12)
(36.538388° -5.358102°)   At this point head slightly right and descend the ridge in front of you for 5 minutes through quite thick undergrowth in places where you then turn left down a very narrow path now crossing a flatter area for a further 5 minutes.

 Pass by three pine trees on your right, before beginning to follow the side of a small valley descending gently. You will pass a fallen tree in the path before crossing the apex and climbing gently the other side. The path leaves the valley and veers slightly left to cross a flatter area with a few trees before arriving at a ruin.

Pass to the right of the ruin, drop down the slope following cairns and white arrows for the next 400 metres as the path disappears in the more open grassy field strewn with stones. You will arrive at a stream bed on your right, at which point you go left to join a wide path in the trees.
(MAP 13) (36.532404° -5.353511°) Turn left again to follow this path up the hill past a pylon and then through a gate. 50 metres later you arrive at the track which brought you to the start of the walk.

WALK 33 - GAUCIN - ASCENT OF EL HACHO FROM THE WEST

Time : 2 hours

Diffculty; hard

Terrain: mainly rough goat paths

Brief description: A spectacular walk , using a path from El Peso rather than the conventional way from Gaucin. Some rock scrambling and very rough paths but well worth the effort .

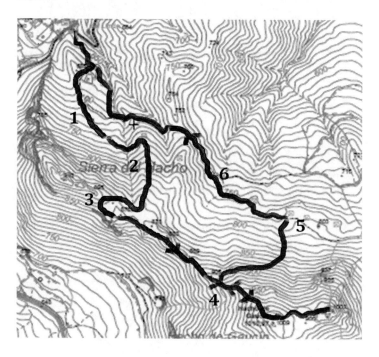

Mapometer showing distances in kilometres

http://gb.mapometer.com/walking/route_4462259.html

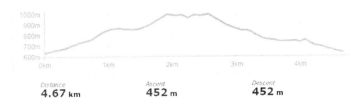

Distance	Ascent	Descent
4.67 km	452 m	452 m

HOW TO GET THERE   Drive from Gaucin on A406 direction Jimena/Algeciras, and after 2 kilometres take the first right turn MA512 to Colmenar/Estación Gaucin; then after 2 more kilometres take a large track sharp right as road bends to the left. Pass over a cattle grid and drive 1 kilometre until you pass through gates (Please shut).   Park at the side of the track as it goes round to the right 50 metres further on.

THE WALK . Just beyond where you have parked the car the track divides . You take the right hand track marked with GR post (red and white) and also with blue stripes . This rough track goes steeply up hill and finishes at a forestry lodge . Leave the GR which heads left of the lodge and go right past a stone plaque saying " IX Via Ferrata Sierra del Hacho " . Follow this route for 5 minutes climbing steeply. Another stone plaque with a IX points to the right . (MAP 1) (36.527651° -5.347798°)

You continue straight on along a widish path which climbs through the trees . At one point you need to veer slightly left off the main path which is about to fizzle out , and follow a rougher path until you can see a pylon in the trees about 50 metres ahead. Look for a fence ahead and as you approach it, turn right up the steep slope keeping the fence on your left and leaving the pylon behind. (MAP 2) (36.526672° -5.345261°) There is also another IX plaque here .

You now have a steep climb for 15 minutes with only goat paths to follow . The easiest way to navigate this section is to keep close to the fence. You will emerge into a grassy area and the fence then turns right and follows along the bottom of a line of craggy rocks which is the ridge of the Sierra del Hacho. You need to go 100 metres to the right , there is a goat path marked with cairns and there will be a wire gate in the fence. (MAP 3) (36.524201° -5.346285°) There is a metal tally to the right of the gate secured to the fence . Pass through, veer left and for the next 10 – 15 minutes you have to make your way along the rocks trying not to drop to far down from the ridge. This rocky outcrop peters out and the mountain slope becomes more wooded and less rocky and climbs more steeply . Note a large white arrow and a cairn atop the last of the outcrops. This is where you turn right on your way back down . (MAP 4) (36.522209° -5.342803°)

Meanwhile continue up on what is now a better path which keeps just to the left of the ridge line and after 10 minutes veers right to pass over to the right of the ridge and the vegetation becomes more thickly covered with tufted grass and scrubby bushes. You are near the top now and you will notice a fence appearing on your left, if you follow the line of the fence it will lead you to the top. Watch out for an unguarded sinkhole near the fence .

At the top there is a trig point and to the north east there is a second peak where there are excellent views down to Gaucin.

To return retrace your steps to the rocky outcrop with the white arrow (MAP 4) (36.522209° -5.342803) to now follow white arrows painted on the rocks. Your direction is north east in a sort of traverse of the hill side gradually losing height . As well as arrows there are frequent cairns some in tree branches . 10 minutes from the ridge you will meet a fence, the path turns left downhill just before the fence.

 At the bottom you will emerge onto a proper path by a gate in the fence. (MAP 5) (36.523956° -5.339757°) Turn left here , you are on the GR 141 which will take you back to the car. The path follows pylons until it passes through a gate emerging onto a wider path .   (MAP 6) (36.525852° -5.342279°) Go left and follow as it passes through a cutting and drops down the side of the hill towards the forestry lodge below.

You pass through one gate and then turn right by a blue paint flash on a low rock then passing a concreted waterhole before 100 metres later arriving at the track you walked up at the beginning of the walk . Your car is at the bottom of the track.

WALK 34- GAUCIN – TO THE LOMO DE MONTORO

Time: 2.5 hours (7 kilometres)

Difficulty: medium

Terrain: road, track, path, some open ground

Brief description: This walk enjoys spectacular views to the north west and mainly passes through council owned land. One part involves an exciting ridge walk through open ground and cork woods .

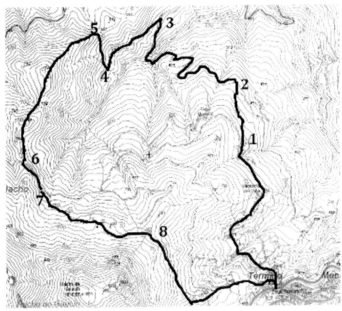

HOW TO GET THERE A369 from Ronda or A405 from Jimena A377 from Sabinillas and park opposite the petrol station.

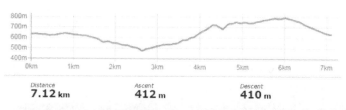

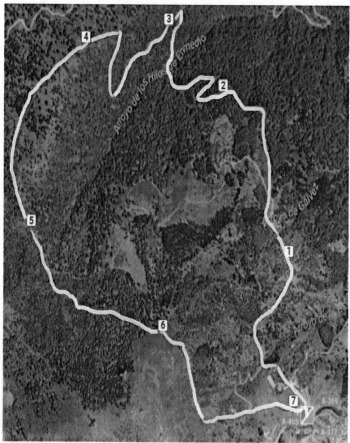

gb.mapometer.com/walking/route_4474122.html

THE WALK

Start at the Gaucin petrol station on the A369/A405. Facing
the petrol station, take the road to the right past some
terraced housing on your right. The road is called Camino el
Montoro.

Follow this tarmac road for about 15 minutes ignoring any
side turnings until you arrive at a collection of farm
buildings. (Disregard a prohibido el paso sign intended for
vehicles) There is a large metal gate across the road which
is normally unlocked . (MAP 1) (36.528085° -5.327803°)
If it is locked there is a wire and post gate to the left. Follow
the road for a few metres before veering right down an
earth track across which is a low chain. Continue down here
for about 200 metres when you will see a fence ahead.
(MAP 2) (36.530912° -5.327858°) Go through a wire
and post gate in front of you and continue down this track
zigagging until you reach the bottom of the valley where you
cross two gullies with streambeds and start rising up the
other side .
About 400 metres from the gullies turn sharp left up a
track. (MAP 3) (36.535162° -5.333422°) Continue until
the track peters out at an open area. (MAP 4)
(36.531594° -5.337944°) Turn and face the way you came
and then go 30 degrees left up through some cork
trees marked by a cairn to join a path by a rock also marked
by a cairn. Follow this path as it rises up towards the ridge.
When you reach a flatter area (MAP 5) (36.535198°
-5.336079°)turn 90 degrees left to climb the ridge towards
its highest point on a rounded knoll. There are some goat
paths to help you but the ground is fairly open along the
top. You will pass over one knoll with giant cork oaks before
dropping down a little before climbing a much steeper and

higher knoll dotted with old cork oaks. Further up there is quite a good goat path leading slightly to the right which avoids the very top of this knoll. Follow this and when you are past the summit, edge round to the left to look for the join between this knoll and the last of the three knolls on this ridge. On this stretch the general gradient is a challengingly stiff climb. You are passing along the boundary between two sections of land owned by the town council marked by occasional signs in the trees saying TRAMO I and II. When you start climbing the last smaller knoll you will see a pylon on the hillside ahead. It is best to traverse on the left side of this knoll following any of the goat paths that abound.

Without losing height and after about 200 metres you should arrive at a gulch/cutting through which passes a good path. (MAP 6) (36.527129° -5.343491°)Turn left onto this path and continue for 200 metres looking for a wire and post gate on the right. (MAP 7) (36.525802° -5.342324°)

Go through and join a narrow footpath snaking its way through the trees and then around the left side of the mountain ahead known as the Hacho . This path follows the line of some pylons .

After 10 minutes pass through a wire and post gate and after a further 500 metres arrive at a flat open area with a pylon. (MAP 8) (36.523107° -5.334584°) Pass through a wire and post gate to your right and head down the hill towards Gaucin which you can see spread out below you. The path reaches a col and turns left to join a narrow track which soon widens a little and passes between two fences to arrive at an open area above the petrol station. You can exit on to the road you began the walk on.

WALK 35- GAUCIN- LA CLARIDAD AND LAS PALAS

Time: 2 hours (7.3 Kilometres)

Difficulty: medium

Terrain: road, path and track

Brief description: a walk that starts on the flat but soon plunges down to the Palas valley and returns through woodland, on the ancient route from Cortes to Gaucin

HOW TO GET THERE Take the A369 from Ronda to Gaucin , A 377 from Manilva to Gaucin or A 405 from Jimena to Gaucin . Park at Petrol Station.

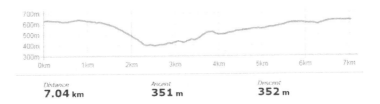

Distance	Ascent	Descent
7.04 km	**351** m	**352** m

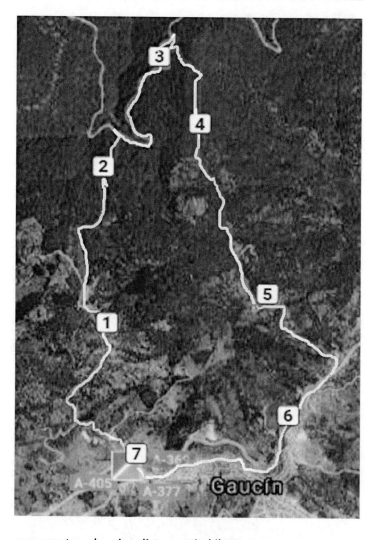

mapometer showing distances in kilometres

http://gb.mapometer.com/walking/route_4458701.html

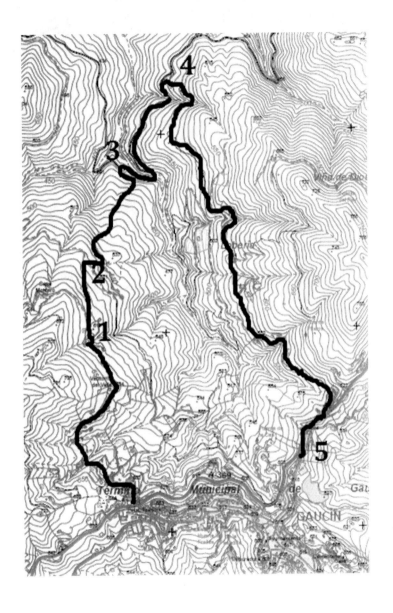

wikilocs route courtesy of Matthew Wolfman

https://www.wikiloc.com/wikiloc/view.do?id=17769780

THE WALK

Start at the Gaucin petrol station on the A369/A405. Facing
the petrol station, take the road to the right past some
terraced housing on your right. The road is called Camino
del Montoro.

Follow this tarmac road for about 15 minutes ignoring all
side turnings until you arrive at a collection of buildings
below you on the right.   You can ignore a sign saying
Prohibido el Paso intended for vehicles. There is a large
metal gate across the road which should be unlocked.
(MAP 1) (36.528085°   -5.327803°) If it is locked go
through a wire and post gate to the left and follow the road
for a few metres before veering right down an earth track
across which is a low chain.

Continue down here for about 200 metres when you will
meet a gate. Dont go through but take the track which
veers round to the right and after 150 metres just the other
side of a gate across the track there is a small wire and post
gate in the fence on the left. (MAP 2) (36.530902°
-5.327411°) In 2017 it has faint turquoise paint flashes.
Pass through and turn immediately right to follow a small
path which after 50 metres turns sharp left to follow a fence
on the right. After a further 50 metres the fence drops away
to the right and you should continue downwards roughly in

the direction you have been following looking for the path as it passes between bushes and bracken .

After 50 metres you pass a large cork oak to your right and and an olive tree to your left. The path then turns right to head straight down the hill. Follow the path down (steep in places) and near the bottom it turns sharp left to reach a wide gravel track. (MAP 3) (36.535173° -5.325726°)

Turn right and follow this track for 10 minutes , crossing one gully with a cattle grid and look for a small path on the right just after a left hand bend.

There will be a black sign with white paint saying "Camino de Gaucín a Cortes" (MAP 4) (36.539569° -5.322740°) marking the path up to the right to Gaucin. The path starts off well defined, turns sharp left and some 80 metres further make sure you turn sharp right by a pine tree as the path splits here. The path continues through magnificent corkwoods with an undergrowth of white heather, sun roses, lavender and broom. On either side there are some spectacular old oaks with wide trunks in strange shapes.

Pass through a wire gate and soon you join a track to continue straight on up the side of the valley passing various farms, some with new houses. The Garganta de las Palas (Garganta means gorge or gully) is below on your right. The track finishes on the Gaucin to Ronda road (MAP 5) (36.524160° -5.313687°) where you turn right to enter the village.

Make sure you have a look at the large notice board on the right showing all the provincial footpaths in the Serrania de Ronda.

WALK 36- GAUCIN CAMINO CORTES AND HEART ATTACK HILL

Time: 2.5 hours (7.5 Kilometres)
Difficulty: medium (one steep climb)
Terrain: track then path , further tracks one section through woods with no apparent path

Brief description: A slightly longer walk with a steep climb through woods , after which there is a gentle return to Gaucin via a highpoint where there are great views to the coast and Africa beyond .

HOW TO GET THERE A 369 to Gaucin. Park at the layby/ mirador at the Ronda end of the village . Walk towards Gaucin.

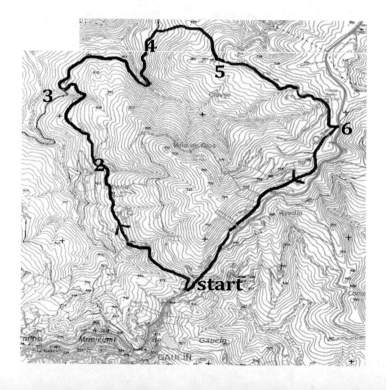

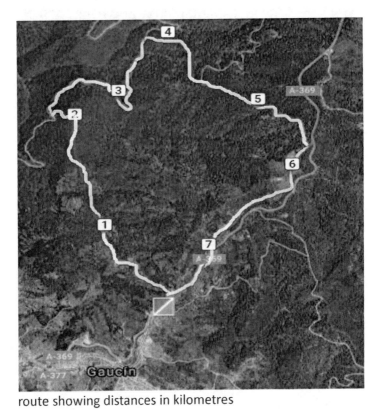

route showing distances in kilometres
link to mapometer
http://gb.mapometer.com/walking/route_4457688.html
link to route on wikilocs courtesy Roger Collinson
https://www.wikiloc.com/wikiloc/view.do?id=16338422

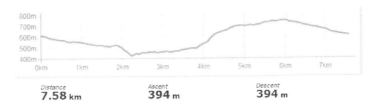

THE WALK

From the layby walk back towards Gaucin and look for a walking map display board on the right hand side of the road before you reach the aviary and bandstand. (MAP 1) (36.524132° -5.313649°) Take the track leaving the road here and pass by a furniture store on the left and a wood yard on the right . The track gently descends on the right side of a valley passing several fincas. After 30 minutes the track turns right into gates to a property. (MAP 2) (36.533477° -5.316419°) You should keep straight on where a path carries on down the hill with a fence on the left. Pass through a gate and follow the path as it traverses woodland eventually arriving at a large pine tree where the path splits. Go left here and you will soon see a large track below. When you reach the track turn right. (MAP 3) (36.539539° -5.322797°)
At this point note your watch as you need to walk for 1200 metres about 15 minutes before you turn off the track to head up into the woods to your right, involving some tricky navigation due to lack of obvious paths.

You are looking for a gap in the undergrowth on the right hand side of a wide gully, above the track just before the track sweeps round the right . (MAP 4) (36.542558° -5.316300°) Prior to this the track has done a sharp left hand turn and is running roughly in a straight line slightly uphill.. There is a goat path which starts to the right of a drainage gully under the track near a tree stump . There is a large cairn placed on the tree stump . The path leads straight up the bank into some large oak trees passing through bushes. Further up you should see the tree featured in the photograph. There is no real path for the next section.

Heart attack hill   photo Roger Collinson

You need to climb straight up here leaving the apex of the
gully to your left and then when the gully appears to veer to
the right and become less steep you also turn right and
continue up hill towards a ridge . There is a large tree with
fallen branches at this point.   Keep to the left of this tree in
the bowl of the gully.   When you reach the ridge
look to the left and there should be path leading to a track
above you.   It does not really matter if you go off course
here . The main aim is to reach the ridge due south of your
direction and then turn left to join the track. (If you are
using the wikilocs track this goes more right and joins the
ridge about 200 metres from the track)

Head up to the left to join the track, hopefully on a corner
where the track bends round to the left . (MAP 5)
(36.541037° -5.310932°) There may be a white paint

mark on the rock above the track on this corner. Turn right here .

Navigation now becomes straightforward :   keep on this track until you reach the main road, ignoring two turn offs to the right, the second opposite a dried up water fountain, and reaching a pair of metal gates . If you have children or dogs take care because the main road is just on the other side of the gates.

Pass through the gates, making sure you leave them shut, then turn immediately right up a small track, next to a large signboard saying "Gaucin, Balcon de la Serranía".(MAP 6) (36.536235° -5.301782°)
On the left is a marker post with a red/white "X" on the post. You can ignore this, as it is indicating that the GR141 route (which goes to Benarraba) goes in a different direction. There is also a yellow/white marker on the same post, and if you look carefully a low rock on the right with a ceramic "VI" sign.   Follow this good track and keep to the left of a pair of large metal gates to Finca 'La Umbria'.

There are fantastic views to the left over the Genal Valley and beyond.   Ignore any side-turnings to private properties and keep on the main track.

As the main road below gets closer, you meet brush-wood gates to a property ahead, and the driveable track ends. Go to the left of the gates on a small narrow path, which goes between between bushes and then descends via a steep rocky gully to the main road. Turn right and return to your starting point.

WALK 37 GAUCIN- CORCHUELO AND JARRAQUEQUE

Time: 2 hours

Difficulty: moderate but one steep scramble

Terrain: tracks , path , a short steep scramble up through woods with no clear path

Brief description: A walk taking in woodland , a vertiginous path along the side of a steep hill , and more gentle track work with great views north up the Genal valley and south past Gaucin towards the coast

HOW TO GET THERE Drive north towards Ronda on the A369 from Gaucin . 2.5 kilometres from the petrol station there is a track off to the right marked with a yellow pillar signed Jarraqueque . Park here .

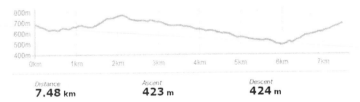

THE WALK

Walk down the track and about 30 metres before a large metal gate across the track, take a narrow path to the left of the main track through shrubs and bushes. (MAP 1) (36.529943° -5.303377°) and after some 20 metres or so pass through a wire and post gate and turn left along an old path that is partly washed away. It runs almost at contour level, but beware of the steep descent to your right. The path runs along pines, Cork oak, Holm oak and through Cistus and other shrubs.

After traversing a gully you arrive at a track as it makes a hairpin bend.

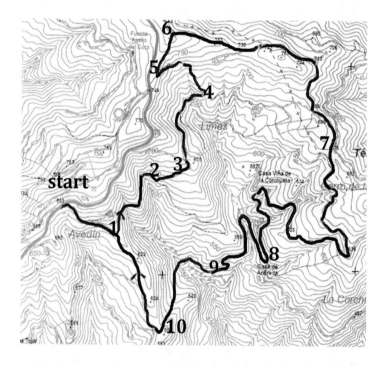

(MAP 2) (36.532333° -5.301321°) Turn left and follow this track as it climbs through woods. After a sharp left hand bend look for a track leading off to the right through a wire and post gate . (MAP 3) (36.533244° -5.299848°)

Take this track which curves round the side of the hill with trees on either side.

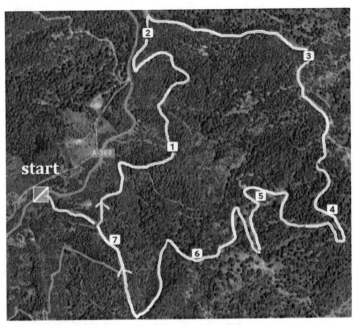

Mapometer showing distances in kilometres
http://gb.mapometer.com/walking/route_4484152.html

wikilocs track courtesy Roger Collinson
https://www.wikiloc.com/wikiloc/view.do?id=16503083

After passing a turn off to the right the track finishes at the foot of a gully . (MAP 4) (36.536082° -5.298798°) A small path continues right, then left up a slope and arrives at a second gully. You need to head up to the left into the trees (there are two large cork trees, cut in 2016 and then pine trees) There is n´t really a path at this point but keep to the left of the gully and climb steeply. You will reach a clump of cork trees and there should be a fence over on the right. Aim for a Y shaped cork tree and just beyond there is the remains of a wide path going slightly left and uphill , a bit overgrown but making life easier. Follow this path for about 50 metres and notice the outline of a track above . Make your way up to this track where there is a concrete well head with a yellow hose running down the hill from where you have just come. Now take this track up the hill, passing a roofless hut on the left. The track levels out and soon on the right there is a path (ignore) and then a wire and post gate marked as the GR141 (red and white flashes) (MAP 5) (36.536733° -5.301645°)

Turn right through the gate and follow the track uphill. At the top pass through a gate (MAP 6) (36.538878° -5.300709°) Turn right and walk along with the fence on your right for about 300 metres until you can join the track below you. Once on the track, continue in the same direction, soon passing one metal gated entrance (Bella Vista) and after 400 metres (5 minutes) a track to the left . 250 metres further there is another gated entrance to the right. (La Corchuela)

Along this section of track you get some impressive views of the valley of the River Genal with the villages of Benarraba, Genalguacil, Jubrique and Cartajima dotted on the hills and the Sierra de las Nieves behind in the far distance. 200 metres from the previous entrance gate, there is a waymarked track going down to the left, which you ignore.

After 50 more metres take the right fork to cross over a cattle grid, (MAP 7) (36.533643° -5.291158°) and then continue along the track as it veers left ignoring the one that goes down to the right immediately beyond the cattle grid. The main track winds its way down through cork trees and pines with views to the Castle of Gaucin, Gibraltar and Africa.

Follow the main track for 700 metres, ignoring a track to the left, where you make an almost 180º turn down to the right. After another 700 metres you will come to a fork. Take the left fork continuing down the track and after 400 metres (5 minutes) take a sharp turn down to the right, crossing over a black water pipe while the main track continues. (MAP 8) (36.528669° -5.294924°) .

After 250 metres, the track makes a sharp left hand bend, crossing a streambed. Continue for 5 minutes ignoring a track up to the right; when the track has completed one zigzag to the left, then right , and on the second zigzag to the left look carefully for and take a small path off to the right marked by a cairn and a green blob on a rock (MAP 9) (36.528272° -5.298236°) After 5 minutes this path enters the gully down to the left containing the Arroyo Higueron meeting a steep wide path coming down the hill from the right . Cross the stream and follow the path as it wends it way up the slope the other side through thickets of tree heather and larger trees . It reaches the ridge where you should look for a wire and post gate just up to the left of a shallow gully where the path appears to lead, to let you into the Jarraqueque estate and you should see a track about 50 metres below . (MAP 10) (36.525756° -5.301339°)Turn right and follow the track ignoring one turn to the left and shortly afterwards arrive at the large gates you saw at the start of the walk . There is a ladder stile to the left . Once over just follow the track back to your car .

WALK 38 GAUCIN - FROM THE GENAL TO LAS LIMAS

Time: 2 hours (5.5 Kilometres) or 7.5 Kilometres from the road
Difficulty: Medium
Terrain: tracks and rough path

Brief description: A walk below Gaucin initially along the Genal river then climbing towards Gaucin and returning across open fields with views up and down the Genal valley.

HOW TO GET THERE   take the A 377 from Gaucin and just before the bridge over the Genal take a steep track down to the left. Either drive 1 kilometre down the track until you cross a ford where the walk starts or park at the start of the track which will add 2 kilometres to your route.

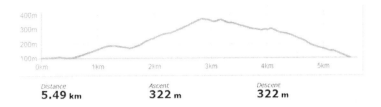

Mapometer showing distances in kilometres

http://gb.mapometer.com/walking/route_4498778.html

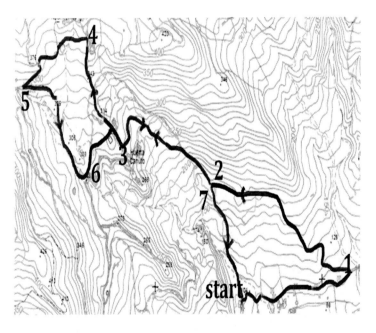

Wiklocs download of walk below
https://www.wikiloc.com/wikiloc/view.do?id=17071151

THE WALK If you have parked near the road then follow the track near the river. The track turns away from the river and up a slight hill then right to pass a house on the right and reaches a ford across a stream. This is the ford where the walk starts.   Pass a few more houses on the right and then look for a wire and post gate on the left (may be open and lying on the ground) about 600 metres from the ford and 200 metres past the last of 5 entrances on the right leading to houses and just past a pylon in a field on the left . (MAP1) (36.501354° -5.298374°)

Go through this gate (may be open) and follow a rough track as it zigzags up the hill before levelling off alongside a wood. You will come to a pile of branches across the track which you need to negotiate followed by a pile of rubble. Immediately take the upper of two tracks and follow. Then take the right hand of two forks and shortly after pass through a wire and post gate. On the other side a lot of clearing has been taking place with some bulldozing as well. Pass some beehives above you and 200 metres further you will come to a turning to the left: 30 metres ahead there is a fence across the track you have been following.   (Map 2) (36.504216° -5.307157°)

Turn left, go 50 metres and turn right through a gate . This track starts to rise passing a track to the left. 50 metres further up a steep rise the track forks , take the left fork , (the right track appears (and is) overgrown). The left track is a bit rough, goes up the hill and becomes a footpath passing the occasional carob tree. After 10 minutes it curves to the left, crosses a stream bed and an uncompleted building should be visible above. You will pass this in a few minutes time. As the path, now more or less a track, approaches a gate , 40 metres before take a

rough path going steeply up to the right (Map 3)
(36.505572° -5.313446°) which will lead you to the
partially built building . Pass by the building leaving it to
your right and just beyond take the left hand path climbing
alongside a low wall to the right . The path is a bit over
grown here . After 5 minutes it joins a track from the left
coming from a finca, you continue uphill. Soon a large villa
will appear on your right. Just past the villa look for a grassy
path to the left up a small bank. Take this path. (Map 4)
(36.509063° -5.315815°) After passing through some large
rocks It drops down and joins a track from the right
leaving a vegetable garden below to the left .

Follow this track briefly into the woods with a finca above
you, before it reverts to a path roughly following the
contour line, overgrown in places. There are several paths
up to the right which you ignore. It crosses a stream at one
point and then meets a grassy track. Turn right, go a few
metres up the slope and this track meets a larger grassy
track coming down the hill.

Turn left down the hill, for 100 metres and take a track to
the left. (Map 5) (36.507518° -5.319945°) Follow for
about 200 metres when it becomes a path, enters some
trees and arrives at two ruins . Pass to the right of the first
ruin, then go left between this building and the next and
down a bank to find a faint grassy path heading down the
hill over open ground . After 5 minutes, at the bottom
ignoring one turn to the right just before the bottom you
arrive at a fence and a track by a water trough.(Map 6)
(36.505017° -5.315582°) Turn left to follow the fence
alongside a rough track . When the fence turns right come
off the track to follow the fence on a small path which
reaches a small orange grove. Just before you reach a

concrete water tank, turn left up through the orange trees up the bank and on the other side you will see the uncompleted building you passed earlier.

Drop down the bank to meet a track . Go right then left by a padlocked gate to rejoin the path on which you came up earlier. (turning right on to this path before reaching the building)
You are now retracing your steps from earlier in the walk . Turn left when you reach the track below and folllow it down the hill for 15 minutes. After you pass through the gate you met earlier go straight down the hill taking a right fork after 70 metres. After you meet a line of trees on your left and just before crossing a streambed leave the track and follow a rough path to the right of the streambed (cairn here) down the hill towards a wire and post gate at the bottom, leading to a track. The ford is 30 metres to your right. Either rejoin your car if here or walk back to the road.

WALK 39- SALITRE - CIRCULAR FROM PUERTO DE LA ERA

Time: 2 hours (6 Kilometres) (9 K if park at main road)
Difficulty: easy
Terrain: mainly tracks, one stretch of open field
Brief description: a relatively gentle walk in the Salitre
valley , a mixture of pasture land and woods with low lying
hills .

HOW TO GET THERE: Take the A369 from Gaucin to Ronda.
After 6 Kilometres turn left on A 373 to Cortes . After just
over 2 Kilometres on a right bend with a bus shelter on the
left , take a concrete track to the left and follow it down hill
ignoring any turn offs for 2.5 kilometres. You will arrive at a
junction of several tracks with a disused chapel ahead. Park
here. If you dont wish to take your car down the track park
at the turn off and walk down. (extra 5 K)

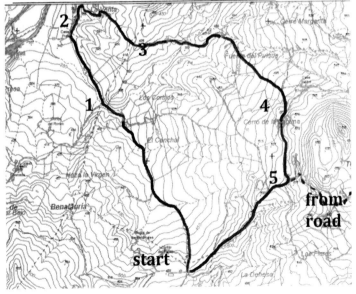

mapometer showing distances in kilometres
http://gb.mapometer.com/route_4516775.html

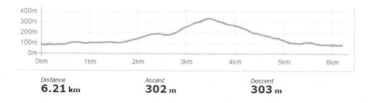

Distance	Ascent	Descent
6.21 km	**302** m	**303** m

THE WALK

Facing away from the track you drove in on, take the right hand track heading down hill. This once driveable track has had serious damage from heavy rains so it is now very rough in places. Lower down it joins a track emerging from a property on the left and becomes easy to walk.

After 1.5 kilometres from the start (25 minutes) you meet a track in front of you. (MAP 1) (36.576561° -5.328528°) Turn right and cross a concrete bridge and continue down this track (the GR 141) for 500 metres until you pass a simple goat farm on the left. (MAP 2) (36.580243° -5.328781°)

Carry on past the farm and after you pass a turn to the left by a couple of houses go 100 metres and take a rough track up to the right which zigzags up past a ruin on your left and continue up the hill passing through scattered trees for about 500 metres from the turning. Look for a wall/fence ahead and there should be a gate in front of you. (MAP 3) (36.580749° -5.325556°) Pass through and join a rough track heading down through the trees.

At the bottom you cross a stream (Arroyo Salitre) and start climbing the other side, passing a cottage on the left. Keep climbing and take the first track to the right after a kilometre (20 minutes) from the stream.(MAP 4) (36.577417° -5.312623°)

Shortly you join a track from the left, turning right at this point. You pass a few houses and farm buildings and the track is then concrete until it meets a track after you climb a slope. (MAP 5) (36.571242° -5.312160°)

Turn right and head downhill ignoring any turn offs to rejoin your car. If you parked at the main road you need to turn left and it is 1.5 kilometres to the road..

40 - SIETE PILAS -SALITRE – GUADIARO CIRCUIT

Time: 3 hours (9 kilometres)
Difficulty: medium
Terrain : tarmac road then track then cross country , track
and rough path

Brief description: A longer walk but with only minor
gradients based on the Guadiaro valley .

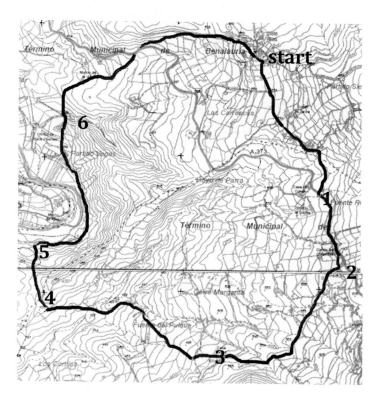

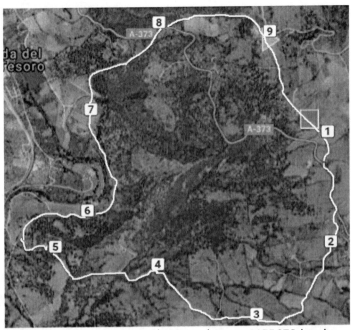

http://gb.mapometer.com/walking/route_4455673.html

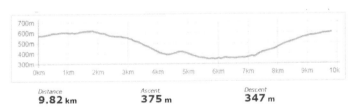

Distance	Ascent	Descent
9.82 km	375 m	347 m

link to wikilocs courtesy of Roger Collinson

https://www.wikiloc.com/wikiloc/view.do?id=16275164

HOW TO GET THERE From the A369 Gaucin to Ronda road take the A373 direction Cortes and after passing the Salitre hotel 1 kilometre further, turn right sign posted to Siete Pilas. This road arrives at an open area with a few scattered houses with the school on the left .

THE WALK   Park outside the school and Medical centre. Walk back along the road you came in on and turn left onto the main road. (MAP 1) (36.588596° -5.302763°) After 250 metres there is a large track off to the right with a couple of wheelie bins in a covered shelter. (MAP 2) (36.584958° -5.301439°)

Follow this track which is concreted in places ignoring numerous side turnings . Your general direction is towards a round hill which you will leave to your left . In more detail there is a right fork after 150 metres, a left fork after a further 150 metres. Soon after the surface becomes gravellled and 15 minutes (1 Kilometre) after the previous fork take a right fork going down hill .   (MAP 3) (36.577790° -5.310194°)

You will pass a finca on your right before fording a stream (the Arroyo Salitre) Keep left at a junction (Right fork is through a padlocked gate) and then gently ascend through olive groves on a rough track which reaches a gate between walls at the crest .(MAP 4) (36.580526° -5.325267°)

Once through the gate go straight on down hill to follow a faint track folllowing the line of trees on your right and an open field which after 150 metres goes into the trees and starts descending. Follow down and when you see a ruin , take a track to the left which leads down to a track below, head for it and turn right. (MAP 5) (36.583457°

-5.330065°) This is part of the GR 141 marked by red and white flashes and you will follow this route until the end of the walk.

This track continues for just under 2 Kilometres passing several farms and fincas . As it crosses more open fields and leaves a few houses on the left (7 Puertas) it then heads down hill and makes a sharp left hand bend.

In front of you there is a house up a slope . (MAP 6) (36.593637° -5.323591°)

Look for a path which passes to the left of this house leaving the main track up to the right. It leads up the slope into trees. It veers right and after 5 minutes it joins a path coming from the left, having passed though a wire and post gate . Turn right and continue until you reach the road . Cross over and take the path opposite, a continuation of the GR 241 .

It climbs the side of the hill and after 1 kilometre you pass a rather ramshackle house on the left and you will soon see the school and chapel ahead . This is Siete Pilas where you left the car.

41 - SIETE PILAS TO ESTACION CORTES

Time; 2 hours (5.9 kilometres)
Difficulty: easy
Terrain: Mainly track , first part is a rough path
Brief description: a gentle walk with kind gradients in the
Guadiaro valley , Follows part of GR 249 and GR 141 ,
Starts in Siete Pilas a tiny hamlet of about 20 houses.

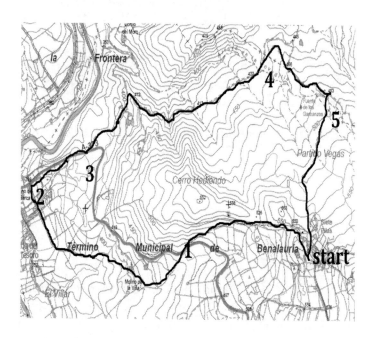

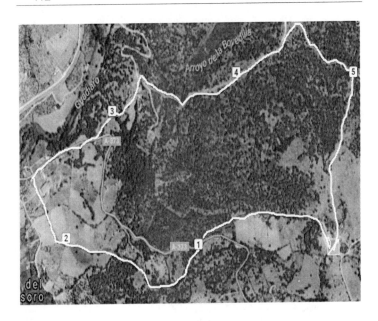

http://gb.mapometer.com/walking/route_4456323.html

Distance	Ascent	Descent
5.86 km	**214** m	**216** m

HOW TO GET THERE From the A369 Gaucin to Ronda road take the A373 direction Cortes and after passing the Salitre hotel 1 kilometre further on, turn right sign posted to Siete Pilas . This road arrives at an open area with a few scattered houses with the school on the left .

THE WALK With the school on your left,   take the left hand of two tracks which curves round past a few houses on the right with one shed on your left. Once past the houses the track becomes a path; you are on the GR 141 which is marked with red and white stripes. The path starts heading down the hill with woods on the right and fields on the left.

After 1 kilometre (15 minutes) you arrive at a road. (MAP 1) (36.598081° -5.317506°) Cross over and take the path opposite (a few metres to the right) which goes down the bank into woods. Follow , ignoring one path to the left which is the GR 141 passing through a gate after 10 minutes. There is a faint yellow and white stripe on a rock on the right at this point. . Ignore one path up to the right through a gate and then pass a house on the right behind a fence. 50 metres past the house the path leaves the woods and enters more open fields in the same direction. In due course it becomes a rough track passing a farm building on the right and then as it arrives at houses becomes a tarmac road.

When it reaches the main road (MAP 2) (36.600907° -5.329635°) turn right to follow for 400 metres where there is a substantial track off to the left . (MAP 3) (36.602371° -5.325051°) Take this track (GR 141A) heading towards Jimera de Libar. After 450 metres passing farms on the left and right the track veers sharp right passing a track to the left .

After a further Kilometre you arrive at a bifurcation. (MAP 4) (36.606324° -5.311766°) Take the right fork which is a lesser track (the main track and GR 141 continues to the left) and after 400 metres the GR 141 and GR 249 appear from the left. 200 metres further on there is a junction. (MAP 5) (36.604977° -5.306584°) Turn right and head up the slope to return to Siete Pilas where your car is parked.

42 SIETE PILAS LAS CANCHAS CIRCUIT
Time: 2 hours (5.4 kilometres)
Difficulty: easy
Terrain: roads rough tracks and paths

Brief description: a gentle walk with the climbing done early in the walk with the rewards of great views soon evident . You pass through two Aldeas. (hamlets)

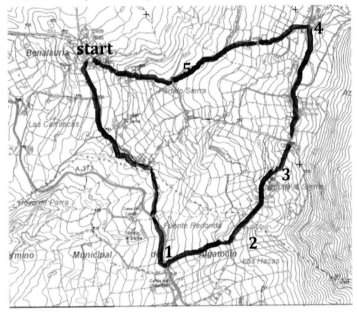

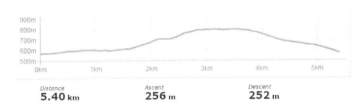

HOW TO GET THERE From the A369 Gaucin to Ronda road take the A373 direction Cortes and after passing the Salitre hotel 1 kilometre further on, turn right sign posted to Siete Pilas. This road arrives at an open area with a few scattered houses with the school on the left.

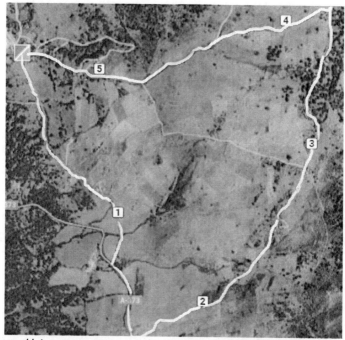

http://gb.mapometer.com/walking/route_4458757.html

THE WALK Park outside the school and Medical centre. Walk back along the road you came in on and turn left onto the main road . Walk 200 metres and just before the entrance to a large track on the right with wheelie bins in a shelter take the entrance to a field where there is an abandoned unfinished house above the road. (MAP 1) (36.585334° -5.301477°) Walk 100 metres up the side of the field moving to the left when you reach a fence in front of you. Now walk on the left side between two fences for 300 metres (5 minutes) until you reach a crossroads of grassy tracks. (MAP 2) (36.586936° -5.297008°) Turn left here through a wire and post gate and go uphill passing through a gate to pass in front of a rustic farmhouse on your right. Take a path just beyond which drops down the slope, passes a spring on the left and then rises up the slope with a tiny stream by the side of the path . You then cross over the stream, pass a large rock on your right, go through a gate and zigzag up the steep bank to pass a further farm house on your right. (MAP 3) (36.590520° -5.293750°) You then join a track leaving the house behind, pass through a metal gate then 100 metres later through another gate to arrive at a cluster of houses along a concrete road . There is a fountain on the right good for topping up water bottles .

Go through this hamlet called Las Canchas and after passing a couple of rustic farmhouses on the left and right look out for a grassy track to the left marked by a GR/PR post with red yellow and white bands. (MAP 4) (36.599557° -5.290917°) Follow this rough, grassy often muddy and stony path down the hill between fences until you emerge onto a quiet tarmac road. Turn left down hill and shortly after passing a traditional looking cottage on the left and as the road bends right, (MAP 5) (36.599557° -5.290917°) go left down a rough path through broom bushes where you soon emerge into a farmyard area full of ramshackle buildings, the odd goat and piles of farm debris. Keeping the house on your left go down a grassy field to join the last part of the path which soon smartens into a paved path arriving at the stone basins of the siete pilas water fountain. You will see your car ahead.

43 SIETE PILAS TO THE CORTIJO PANRICO

Time : 2.5 hours (8 Kilometres)
Difficulty: medium
Terrain: first part on tracks then a rough path and finally track and tarmac

Brief description: A walk with great views of the Guadiaro valley climbing to 800 metres, passing through some remote fincas before gently descending via a tarmac road to the start. mapometer showing distances in kilometres

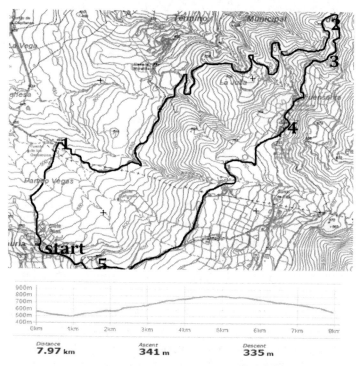

http://gb.mapometer.com/walking/route_4458757.html

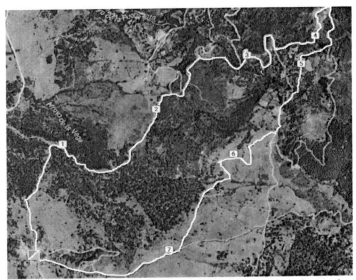

HOW TO GET THERE From the A369 Gaucin to Ronda road
take the A373 direction Cortes and after passing the Salitre
hotel 1 kilometre further on, turn right sign posted to Siete
Pilas. This road arrives at an open area with a few scattered
houses with the school on the left. Park here

THE WALK Keeping the school on your left walk down the
track taking care to take the right hand of the two tracks
ahead. Head down the hill (this is the GR 249 and 141)
until you reach a junction at the bottom. (MAP 1)
(36.604795° -5.306537°) Turn right and follow this track
as it winds up the hill. Ignore any left turnings. The first
left turning has a sign board advertising horse riding. The
second is an actual bifurcation but keep right here and keep
climbing. Shortly after this fork the track does two sets of
zigzags and soon there is a wooden barred gate on the
right side with a privado sign to the left of the gate. Ignore
this entrance. Continue for 600 metres after this and as
you approach a wooded area above the track there is a

rough track off to the right. (MAP 2) (36.613809°
-5.285889°) Take this and walk 300 metres and look for a
small path off to the right. (At the time of writing it is
obscured by debris from   felled pine trees so until cleared
away it will be a question of picking your way through
heaidng down the slope until you can locate the path the
other side of the felled trees. The start is just a few metres
beyond what looks like a tiny quarry with a rockface on the
left hand side. (MAP 3) (36.611388° -5.285991°)
The path plunges down briefly before levelling out to
follow the contour line between two fences , then climbing
and then dropping down to pass right in front of a finca
owned by a german family . Dont worry that you are
passing so close, The author has been reassured by the
owner (Juli) that this is the correct path.   Having passed the
finca and a modern looking house behind you continue
along a path passing a track to the right.   At this point pass
through a wooden barred gate and take the path as it runs
between two walls. (MAP 4) (36.607747° -5.289093°)
Cross a stream and head upwards towards another finca
pasing this one to your right on what is now a track and
after passing another finca on your left then meet a larger
track. Turn right and follow this track down the hill. It
does large loops and it is possible to cut the corners by
crossing over the open ground.   It then becomes tarmaced
and meets the GR 249 coming in from the left.   Shortly after
passing a house on the left the track/road bends to the
right . (MAP 5) (36.596483° -5.303277°) You go straight
on down a grassy path through broom bushes to a
ramshackle farm.   Leave it to your left taking a rough path
straight on down the hill which will take you back to your
car.

44 ESTACION DE CORTES CIRCUIT

Time: 2 hours (6 kilometres)
Difficulty: easy
Terrain: track and road

Brief Description: this is an easy walk with hardly any
climbing, along either side of the Rio Guadiaro, and
walking the length of Estacion De Cortes (Cañada del Real
Tesoro)

HOW TO GET THERE   From A369 take the A373 direction
Cortes and after you cross the river at Estacion de Cortes
park in the road running alongside the railway on your right.

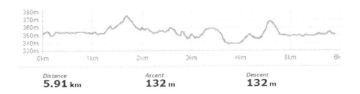

THE WALK   Walk back over the bridge and take the first
track on the right.   You pass by a few houses and then enter
flat countryside with fields either side and the occasional
finca. After 20 minutes you make a sharp right hand turn up
a hill with a very garish green facaded house on the left.
Here you join the GR 141 which emerges on a path form the
left .   You then pass through a community known as 7
puertas .   Ignore any turnoffs remaining on the main track
until it passes quite close to the river. About 10 minutes
after it leaves the river rising a little, there is a turning near a
house which leads down to the river.   Turn right (MAP 1) (
36.582892° -5.330548°) There is a footbridge here not

initially visible but round the corner past a house on the left.
Cross over the river and arrive at a small tarmac road.
(MAP 2) (36.584376° -5.332103°)

Turn right and follow this road all the way back to the village
. Past a small school on the left look for a side street which
will take you up to a square with new houses and the small
town hall at the top. Follow the street round to the right to
walk alongside the railway when you will meet the main
road at the level crossing.   Your car should be down the
road ahead

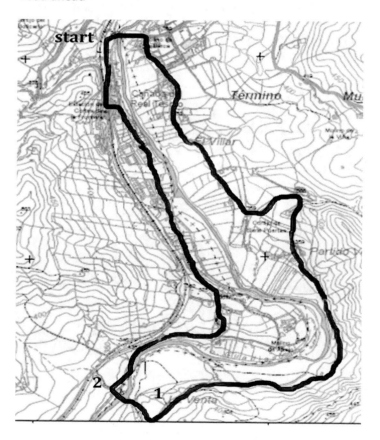

http://gb.mapometer.com/walking/route_4467551.html

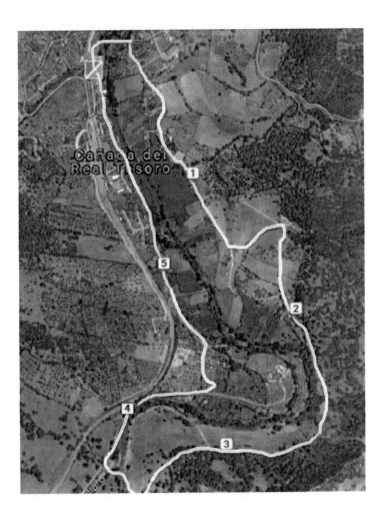

45 BENARRABA TO LAS HAZUELAS

Time: 2 hours (6.5 kilometres)
Difficulty: easy
Terrain: mainly tracks one rough path

Brief description: A gentle walk starting from Benarraba,
with good views over the Genal valley.

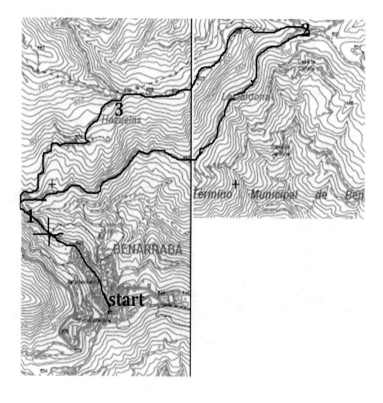

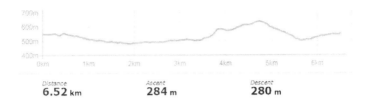

Mapometer link
http://gb.mapometer.com/walking/route_4456360.html

HOW TO GET THERE . Turn off the A369 Gaucin to Ronda road 4 kilometres north of Gaucin. Park at entrance to village of Benarraba.

THE WALK On the left as you enter the village there is Bar Guayacan on the corner. Veer left past the bar and take Calle Tolledillo . Continue along this street until the far end of the village when it becomes a track and head west out of the village. The track descends slightly and crosses a stream turning sharp right in the process. Shortly afterwards there is a junction (MAP 1) (36.555112° -5.280985°) Take the right fork and continue for 2 kilometres (30 minutes) on this flat track following the 500 metre contour line. 50 metres past a turn off to the right take a track to the left. (MAP 2) (36.562181° -5.262713°) Then, after a few metres the track splits: take the left which dwindles away to a rough path climbing the ridge.

Follow this rough path keeping in the middle of the ridge up the steepish slope until it joins a track from the right coming from a finca. Follow this track with a fence on your right for about 500 metres passing a farm which may have loose animals including chickens and goats.

You will arrive at a junction of tracks by a pylon. (MAP 3) (36.559441° -5.275121°) Take the left track and follow it, ignoring one turn off to the right after a few metres. You descend gently for about one kilometre (15 minutes) until you arrive at the junction at MAP 1 .

Turn right here and retrace your steps back to the village .

46 BENARRABA- NORTHERN CIRCUIT

Time: 2.5 hours (9 kilometres)
Difficulty: medium
Terrain: mainly tracks, one steep descent on a rough path ,and a further section on a narrow path.

Brief description: a longer walk but not too taxing as the ascent is gentle up a track. There are views up and down the Genal Valley and back towards Benarraba

HOW TO GET THERE   Turn off the A369 Gaucin to Ronda road 4 kilometres north of Gaucin. Follow signs to hotel and park at the far end of the village by the school.

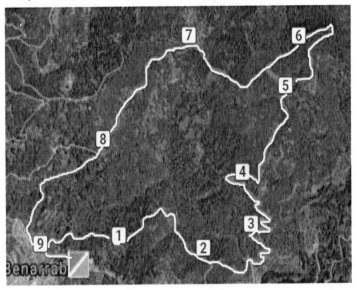

Mapometer showing distances in kilometres

http://gb.mapometer.com/walking/route_4456412.html

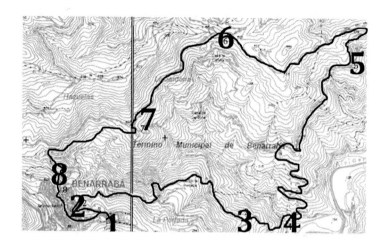

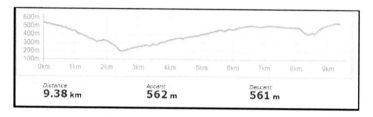

Distance
9.38 km

Ascent
562 m

Descent
561 m

THE WALK walk back with the school on your right and
take the right hand street going down the hill. (Av Miguel
Perez Delgado) (MAP1) (36.550959° -5.272990°)
Towards the bottom take the first street on the right (Calle
Sol) which drops a little further down, bends sharp right
and starts flattening out and bending to the left. On the
right there is a panel illustrating a walking route the first
part of which you will be following. (MAP 2) (36.551478°
-5.275303°) Turn right down a gravel track which will
descend the hill for about 2 kilometres (20 minutes or so)
before you leave it to take a path down to the river. (MAP
3) (36.551018° -5.262316°)

This path is off to the left after the track has levelled off and then risen a little. The path, steep in places, arrives at the foot of the hill into a flat area and crosses a stream(bed) before arriving at a track. (MAP 4) (36.550923°
-5.258471°)

Turn left and follow this track as it starts to rise up the hill zigzagging from time to time, passing side tracks which you ignore making sure you stay on the main track. As the track begins to level out there is a turn down to the right through gate posts (no gates); (MAP 5) (36.560475°
-5.253229°) ignore this and soon after your track makes a hairpin bend to the left and heads south west following the contour line.

After one kilometre from the hairpin bend and after passing two tracks off to the right, the track makes a gentle curve to the left; ignore one prominent track off to the left going down hilland one up to the right. Your track remains following the contour line . (MAP 6) (36.562163°
-5.263198°)

Almost exactly 1 kilometre (15 minutes from this last fork the track bends to the right and there is a track off to the left on a promontory . (MAP 7) (36.556586° -5.270917°) Leave the main track, turn left and immediately right where a rough track heads down the slope and appears to peter out in a flat grassy patch. At the far end take a very small rough path continuing in the same direction clinging to the side of the hill. It will arrive at a stream in a gully. Cross and the path then begins to climb passing a few fincas on either side. You then arrive at the edge of the village. (MAP 8)
(36.552191° -5.276362°)

There are several ways back but to enjoy the main sights turn right up the first street Calle Sausal then left up Calle Posito past the town hall and the church. The street becomes Calle Calzada and at the top you turn left down the street you drove in on passing a square with the ermita at the far end . The school is 100 metres further on. There is a bar just past the school for refreshments, part of the hotel Banu rabbah .

47 BENARRABA- SOUTHERN CIRCUIT

Time: 2 hours (5.2 kilometres)
Difficulty: medium
Terrain: tracks and two steep paths

Brief description : A varied walk with woodland and valley,
and a visit to a ruined mill. Some steep climbs in places.

HOW TO GET THERE . Turn off the A369 Gaucin to Ronda
road 4 kilometres north of Gaucin. . Park at entrance to
village of Benarraba.

wikilocs track courtesy of Roger Collinson
https://www.wikiloc.com/wikiloc/view.do?id=16628716

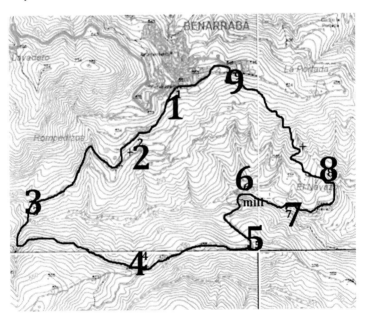

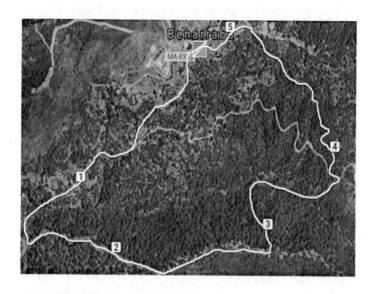

route showing distances in kilometres
link to route in mapometer
http://gb.mapometer.com/walking/route_4456421.html

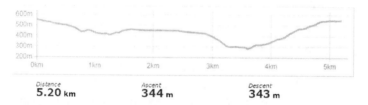

Distance
5.20 km

Ascent
344 m

Descent
343 m

THE WALK

On the right hand corner as you enter a flat area with a few parked cars and a bar on the left called GuayaCan take the track/road down to the right where you will find a board indicating a few paths, amongst them: PR A 243 GAUCÍN 3h, RIO GENAL 1h:45min, GENALGUACIL 2h:45min and the GR

141.   From here follow the signs to Gaucín. (MAP 1)
(36.549959° -5.276041°)
Follow the main track down that runs in between farms,
agaves and prickly pears, with the Sierra Bermeja present on
your left.   Further down on the left 20 metres beyond the
old wash basins of the village continue down the main road
and then soon, on a hairpin bend to the left, you turn right
(following the signpost to Gaucín). Pass through the metal
gates of Finca Gaspara and continue down the track. On
your track there are white red and yellow flashes on a fence
post on the left hand side of the track. The track gently
descends between fences on either side passing one
building on the right.

 Stay on the main track and eventually   the track, with a
gate ahead, does a sharp bend to the left where there is a
post with a cross on   - which you leave - your path to the
right, is hardly visible, very narrow − it is between the
track just mentioned and a wire and post gate on the right -
dropping steeply past a large oak tree keeping a fence to
your right, (it is waymarked) towards the stream of La
Vegueta (it can be muddy here). (MAP 3) (36.543162°
-5.281996°) Cross the stream, heading left and up the
slope to join a more substantial grassy track that you follow
to the left. Further on you can see the villages of
Genalguacil and Jubrique appearing above the edge of the
forest. After forking left at the point where the GR141
veers right up the hill towards Gaucin and continuing for
about 500 metres you arrive at a junction of tracks . (MAP
4) 36.540677° -5.278296°).

 Go half left to follow a track which rises up a ridge then
follows it .

After about 600 metres, watch out for a path going steeply down to the left. (MAP 5) (36.541700° -5.271645°) It's not that obvious, but look out for a large oak, next to the start of the path. At the top there are two large cork trees the second of which has a cairn at its base.   The path is in poor condition, due to deep runnels caused by rain. It is a beautiful shaded path through broom, heather and mixed woodland.

Eventually you reach the bottom of the valley and arrive at the ruins of an old watermill. (LA MOLINETA) (MAP 6) (36.544474° -5.272407°) There is detailed information on the history and workings of the mill on a display board. Beyond this mill keep on the right side of the stream on a path which follows the stream.   After about 400 metres you arrive at a junction. (MAP 7) (36.543865° -5.269425°) Take the left hand path which drops down and crosses the stream. The path then zig zags steeply up the hill to meet a gravel track. (MAP 8) (36.544949° -5.268130°)
Cross straight over and take the path up into the trees and you will immediately emerge at the junction of a track and a couple of paths. Pass between a pair of large concrete manhole covers,   and directly ahead you will see a substantial oak tree with a single rock cairn at its base with a painted Red/White flash. Take the smaller left hand path and continue steeply upwards. It is a stiff climb up a path which over the centuries has worn a deep furrow between its banks. You will arrive just in front of the village school. (MAP 9)   (36.550774° -5.272697°)
Turn left to reach the centre of Benarrabá and your car. Coming first to a square, continue through to reach Bar GayaCan and the road out of Benarraba where you left your car.

48 BENARRABA TO BENESTAPAR

Time: 2 hours (6.5 Kilometres)
Difficulty: Hard due to steep and overgrown path
Terrain : Small paths overgrown in places , river crossing ,
track to finish.

Brief description: This is a challenging walk due to tricky
navigation , a river crossing and overgrown path. A walk for
the more adventurous . Do not attempt after heavy rain as
the river will be too swollen to cross.   However a rewarding
walk as you enter remote and beautiful countryside you
would never otherwise see.

HOW TO GET THERE Turn off the A369 Gaucin to Ronda
road to Benarraba . AS you arrive in the village with Bar
Guayacan on the left turn sharp right where there are a
cluster of signs for various footpaths . Follow this tarmac
road down hill for two kilometres until just when the
tarmac finishes abd there are footpath signs on either side .

Park here .

THE WALK continue to a left hand bend where there is a
pylon and look for a footpath sign to the right and take this
path down the hill zigzagging .   There is a display panel
describing the path called Concoste la Porta.   Once across
the stream at the bottom go up the other side and turn left
onto a path coming down the valley . (MAP1) (36.543790°
-5.269463°)

Follow the path as it skirts round the hill and ignore one left
fork.

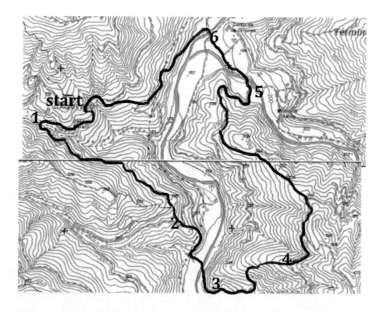

Eventually it drops steeply down to a track. (MAP 2)
(36.538203° -5.259806°) Cross over and continue down
the narrow path. You will come to another track. Here turn
right and follow as it curves left down to the river
deteriorating to a wide path between two fences .

At the river cross at the ford and take the track uphill the
other side. Pass through a gate ignoring the prohibido el
paso sign intended fro vehicles (see Rafa Flores book Valle
del Genal which has part of this walk in it) This is a fertile
little corner of the Genal with a house on the right. As the
track bends to the right and 30 metres before gate posts
there is a track to the left which only goes a few metres
before becoming a small path bending to the right up the
steep slope. (MAP 3) (36.534871° -5.257081°) Follow

this path as it zizags up the hill and then heads north to a ridge where it veers right to follow the ridge uphill. (In 2016 this path has been cleared to enable the cork to be extracted .)

After 5 minutes take a right fork (not obvious) and continue climbing. Then take a left turn onto a path ascending from the right between eroded banks .

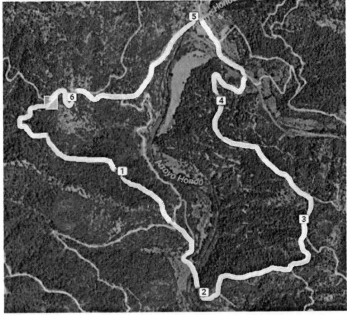

http://gb.mapometer.com/walking/route_4474398.html

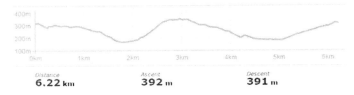

At this point notice a tree stump on your right with a number 6 pinned to the stump.

Soon the path is blocked by fallen tree branches and you need to veer right to avoid this obstacle. The path turns right to rejoin the ridge here so follow for only 5 metres where there is a fork. Take the right fork which again goes straight on up the ridge meandeirng a little to circumvent the numerous pine and cork trees growing on the slope. Basically your route is to follow the ridge straight up making sure you dont leave the ridge.

Soon there is a fence on your left and 100 metres further up you pass through a wire and post gate. Continue uphill on the path and you will join a rough track emerging from your left. There is now an olive grove on your right and you follow this rough track making sure you keep the olive grove on your right for 100 metres until you reach a driveable track. (MAP 4) (36.536108° -5.252663°) Turn left and after 250 metres you join another track. Turn left and follow the track down hill past one track on the right and then a newish house on the right. Ignore any turnoffs and you will curve round to the right and drop down towards a river (Almarchal) below. As the track reaches the river turn left down a side track and cross the river over some stepping stones . (MAP 5) (36.546207° -5.255600°) Then follow the river bank until you join a rough track which soon arrives at an open area with picnic tables and a childrens climbing frame .

At the far end is the river Genal. Cross over using a concrete bridge and turn left (MAP 6) (36.548903° -5.258288°)up a good track which climbs up the hill. After passing one track to the left then another to the right, the track does a loop to the left and passes a pylon on the left where your car should be parked.

49 ALGOTOCIN LAS PILAS CIRCUIT

Time : 1.5 hours (4.6 Kilometres)
Difficulty: easy
Terrain: paths and tracks , one steep path up

Brief Description: a shorter walk based on Algotocin ,
rewarded with great views over the Genal valley. Once you
have completed the steep initial climb the walk is on gentle
tracks and paths .

HOW TO GET THERE Algotocin is on the A369 Gaucin to
Ronda road . Park at the entrance to village on the side road
to Jubrique and Genalguacil and head to the main square
Alameda de Andalucia .

THE WALK facing up hill take the right hand street going up
to the right of the Post Office, take the first left at the Banco
de Santander then head up to the main road past the Health
Centre. Turn right onto the road and look for a steep stone
paved track heading up hill on the left signposted to the
Ermita del Santo Cristo .   (MAP 1) (36.573715°
-5.276352°)

At the first white building take the path off to the left
passing to the right of the building , (the stone track
continues to the right up to the Ermita, worth a detour for
the views .)

Once back on the dirt path continue climbing for about 20
minutes when you emerge in front of the Las Pilas water
source known as the Fuente de San Isidro. Turn right here

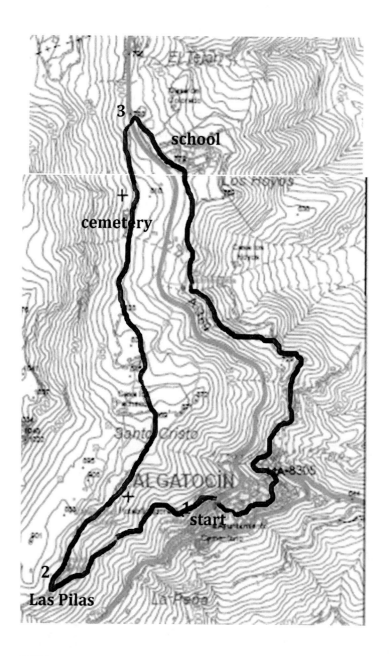

to follow a track passing several fincas and finally the new cemetery before emerging onto the main Ronda road.

Cross over and take the road which leads to the car park for the area secondary school (instituto). Look for a track/path leading off to the right as the tarmac road heads to the school which then follows parallel to the road above on the right. The track narrows to become a path and passes a spring (Fuente de Sementillos).

20 minutes after leaving the school the path reverts to a concrete road and starts to pass scattered buildings and enters the outskirts of Algotocin.   Carry on into the village passing a small apartment block (Boquea A).   Turn left at a pylon shortly afterwards and continue uphill. Take Calle Perez Jimenez, pass Supermercado Duarte, then turn left down Avenida de Andalucia to return to the main square where there are bars for refreshments .

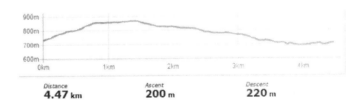

Distance	Ascent	Descent
4.47 km	**200** m	**220** m

http://gb.mapometer.com/walking/route_4456971.html

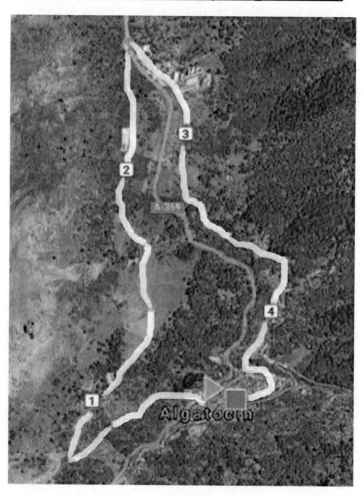

50 ALGOTOCIN TOWARDS BENARRABA

Time: 2.5 hours (7.8 Kilometres)
Difficulty: Medium
Terrain: Mainly tracks, one path and short section of road

Brief Description: an attractive route between Algotocin and Benarraba using old tracks connecting the two villages .

HOW TO GET THERE Algotocin is on the A369 Gaucin to Ronda road . Park at the entrance to the village on the side road to Jubrique and Genalguacil and head towards the main square Alameda de Andalucia .

THE WALK

Dont enter the square but continue on the Calle Jubrique to the right and 50 metres later take a narrow concrete track to the right by the cemetery just beyond two wheelie bins.
(MAP 1) (36.572405° -5.276859°   It soon turns right then left then right again and after passing a solitary building on the left becomes a narrow rocky path descending in zigzags. It curves round the side of a hill and into a gully which it crosses and edges round the other side climbing a little.

You then join a grassy track emerging from the right and which continues on the contour line passing a sollitary house on the left.

It starts climbing and as you pass a gate on the left with the initials JPM in metal, turn right at a junction and

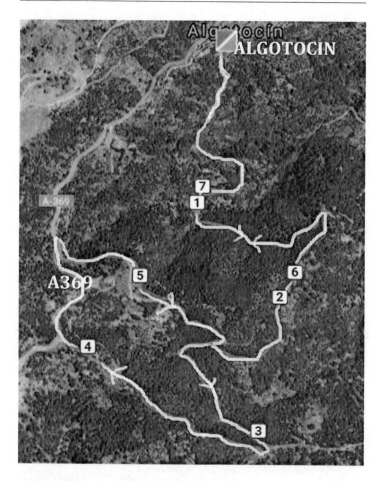

Map showing kilometre markers

http://gb.mapometer.com/walking/route_4456355.html

For wicilocs track see
http://www.wikiloc.com/wikiloc/view.do?id=16162582
(Algatocín - Lower Circular) at #wikiloc   Courtesy of Roger
Collinson

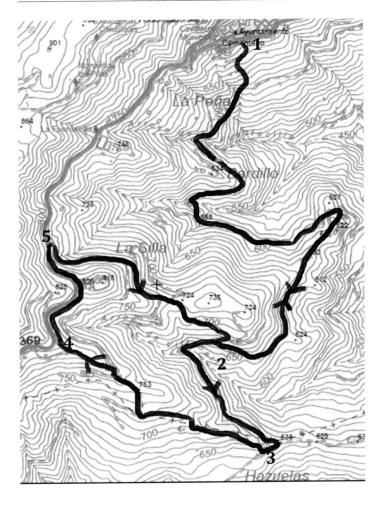

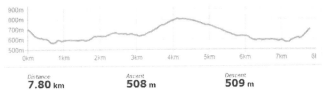

continue up the hill. When you arrive at another junction
with finger posts to the left and the right (the left one is
missing its sign) turn left . (MAP 2) (36.562783°
-5.277520°) (You will later return on the track up to the
right signposted Algotocin) Follow this track down hill for
500 metres where there is another junction by a pylon on
the right. Turn right here (there is a big white arrow
pointing this way on a concrete base at the foot of the
pylon) (MAP 3) (36.559459° -5.275158°)

Go about 150 metres and take a sharp right turn at the next
junction. On the left just before this junction there is a
finger post indicating a cycle route Descenso 700 metres
BTT. Head up this steep track passsing a finca on the left by
a right hand bend. Ignore one track off to the left heading
into woods. Your route arrives at a ridge by a ramshackle
finca with many pallets used for fencing. The track is now
concreted and arrives at the main road after a few minutes.
(MAP 4) (36.562905° -5.283503°) Turn right and follow
the road for 400 metres making sure you visit the excellent
Mirador on the right after 200 metres. 200 metres further
on turn right (MAP 5) (36.566034° -5.283670°) down a
steep gravel track and follow for about 1 kilometre.

Then turn left to rejoin the track you were on earlier to
return to Algotocin along the route you came out on. (MAP
2) (36.562798° -5.277501°)

51 GENALGUACIL- AROUND THE ALMARCHAL

Time: 2 hours

Difficulty: medium

Terrain: paths and tracks

Brief Description: a very varied walk starting from the picturesque village of Genalguacil, plunging down to the Rio Almarchal before climbing back up along the GR 249.

HOW TO GET THERE Turn off the A369 at Algotocin and follow signs to Genalguacil. Park at entrance to village.

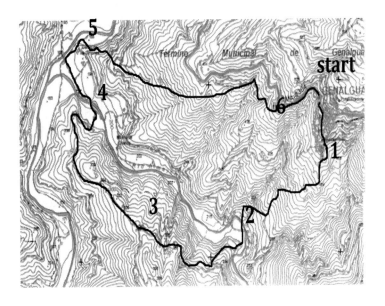

track as shown on wikilocs link below

https://www.wikiloc.com/wikiloc/view.do?id=16535413

THE WALK :   Head into the village along the main street
(Calle Real) The village is noted for its street art , mainly
sculptures and there is a museum. At the end by the church
drop down right to the Plaza to enjoy the views towards the
Genal valley. Return to the Calle Real and just beyond the
end of the church take a concrete track down to the right
(MAP1) (36.544297° -5.235578°) and after a few metres
swing right to follow a footpath sign. (Puerto de Lentisco)
Pass Finca Bancaliyo and drop steeply down hill keeping to
the main path.   As the path widens you should hear the
river below. The track meets another track, turn right and
after a hairpin left you arrive at the river. There will be a
ruined bridge a little upstream and a farm on the left.
(MAP 2) (36.538575° -5.242678°) Cross the river and

before you reach the ruined bridge look for a path in the bushes heading up the slope. There are yellow and white markers to help you. This narrow path climbs steeply away from the river amongst prickly pears.

You will join a track bearing right to continue up and eventually level off to meet another track by an abandoned farmhouse. (MAP 3) (36.539736° -5.251582°) Turn right here and follow it down hill past a house and buildings on the right. The track loops to the right before approaching the river again. As it hits the river turn left down a track which soon peters out. (MAP 4) (36.546096° -5.255583°) Cross the river here and on the other side follow the bank of the river until you come to an open grassy area with a few picnic tables around the edge. At the far end is the Rio Genal where there is a road crossing. On the right there is a house with a large stone wall. At the end of the wall by the river crossing there is a footpath finger post indicating the GR 249 and GR 141. Head upstream signposted Benalauria and Genalguacil and after 50 metres go up the bank to the right to follow the GR 249 footpath to Genalguacil. (MAP 5) (36.549359° -5.257153°) It is welll marked with red and white signs.

After 5 minutes cross over a track into cork oaks and soon cross another track. The path is easy to follow until you reach the main road. It curls round a gully with the crash barrier of the road 20 metres above at one stage before joining a track by a basketball court to arrive at the road. (MAP 6) (36.546197° -5.239694°) Turn right to return to Genalguacil. There is a venta at this junction for refreshments .

WALK 52- GENALGUACIL AND UP THE GENAL

Time: 2.5 hours (8 Kilometres)
Difficulty: medium
Terrain: paths and tracks

Brief description: a varied walk, with woodland, stretches of river, valley views and metal walkways, slightly longer but worth the extra effort.

HOW TO GET THERE Turn off the A369 at Algotocin and follow MA8305 and signs to Genalguacil. The road forks right after crossing the river Genal . Park at entrance to village.

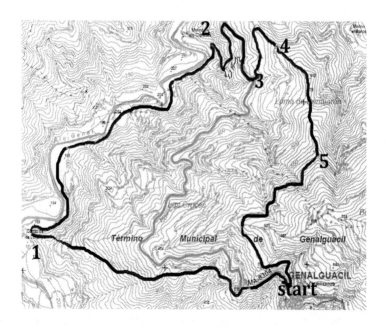

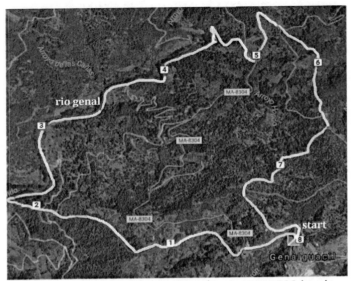

http://gb.mapometer.com/walking/route_4455638.html

Distance	Ascent	Descent
8.12 km	**509** m	**503** m

THE WALK . Walk back along the road you drove in on and opposite a venta on a right hand bend take a track to the left leaving a tennis court / basketball court on your right . Take the waymarked footpath to the right. This path will have red/yellow/white flashes marking the way down the hill as far as the river. (GR 249 and PR A 240). The path roughly follows a ridge and will cross two tracks on the way down. Just before the path reaches the bottom you pass a house on the left. (MAP 1) (36.549402° -5.257055°)At the river turn right and join the GR 141 /249 which will now follow the river upstream using metal walkways where the cliffs abut the river. This is a very attractive part of the walk.

You will be aware of riverside fincas from time to time. After 20 minutes or so on the river path and after you descend from a metal walkway you arrive at a driveable track. (MAP 2) (36.559087° -5.242036°) Turn right and follow the track uphill until you arrive at a tarmac road. Turn right and follow the road for 350 metres passing Kilometre marker 2 and then on a right hand bend take the steep track to the left through a pair of metal gates. (MAP3) (36.557625° -5.238601°) If the gates are padlocked there is a path in the ditch to the left. Proceed up the track passing a finca on the right. The track bends to the right, you ignore a steep track down to the left and you pass another finca on the right. (There are great views towards Jubrique on your left) 100 metres later you reach a junction of tracks . (MAP 4) (36.559541° -5.236742°) Between the two tracks, at the start of the left hand track on the right , look for a path climbing up the bank in front of you. It starts a few metres down the left track. As it climbs steeply you pass a circular brick water tank and then the path enters woods with eroded banks on either side. It emerges onto a ridge, flattens out before passing a derelict barn on the left .

You approach woodland again ; stay on the main path ignoring a fork to the left and you will climb steeply through the woods . Look out for a house above you and the path will pass round the back to join the access track near the swimming pool beyond the house . You pass a finca on the left and then shortly you will arrive at a well maintained track . (MAP 5) (36.553522° -5.233591°) Turn right and folloow the PR 241 from Jubrique to Genalguacil which will be marked with yellow and white flashes. Continue, ignoring all side turnings, until you arrive in Genalguacil where you need to turn right to reach the lower road where your car is parked .

WALK 53 BENALAURIA - SENDERO LAERAS TO MAYORDOMA

Time: 1.5 hours 4.7 kilometres

Difficulty: easy

Terrain: rough path and tracks

Brief description: A shortish walk but a very attractive one, crossing a small valley with a couple of streams then passing down a ridge before plunging down to cross the arroyo de las Veguetas to return to Benalauria.

HOW TO GET THERE   take the A 369 from Gaucin towards Ronda and after Algotocin take the road down to Benalauria. Park at the entrance of the village on the lower road .

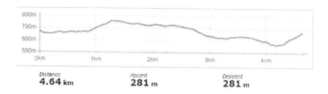

Distance
4.64 km

Ascent
281 m

Descent
281 m

Link to wililocs (Courtesy Roger Collinson)

http://www.wikiloc.com/wikiloc/view.do?id=16204657

http://gb.mapometer.com/walking/route_4450237.html

THE WALK Walk towards the village and at the end of the car park on the left there is a set of steps. (MAP 1) (36.595343° -5.261074°) Go down here and descend to a concrete road. Turn left and follow as it leaves the village on the level. It passes a wash house on the left and then becomes a path. It stays on the level for a while crossing a stream on a wooden bridge and then crossing a second stream a few minutes later .

 At this point the path splits. There is a yellow painted tile on the bank behind the path shaped to point left. (MAP 2) (36.597958° -5.267253°) Go left here and the path starts zigzagging up the hill passing at one point a pretty tile illustrating the ubiquitous olive tree just before a left bend. Eventually you emerge on to a driveable track with a plaque opposite saying sendero laeras . (MAP 3) (36.600327° -5.266603°)

Turn right here and follow this track down the ridge ignoring one turn to the right and a second right turn further down. After 20 minutes on this track and having admired the impressive views on either side look for a turn off to the right liberally adorned with white markers and a broken PR post (yelllow and white) which has been lodged up the bank on the right . (MAP 4) (36.601053° -5.250963°)

A combination of white markers and yellow and white flashes will guide you back to Benalauria along this very pretty track, then path. The path plunges down to the Arroyo Vegueta which you cross before toiling up steeply to the village.

Benalauria is one of the most attractive villages in the Genal valley with no ugly development on the edges . To see more of the village and to make it a genuine 2 hour walk I suggest you take the first street to the left when you arrive at the village and follow the street all round the bottom. As you then start leaving the village on a concrete track and past the last uncompleted building on the right take a narrow path just beyond which curls round and up the side of the hill. Then keep taking left turns to get to the top of the village to get great views of the valley . And when you reach the top street you can either take a path to the left up to the Torre (tower) (sign posted) or head down to the right into the square where there is bound to be a bar open.

<u>Things of interest in Benalauria</u>

Ethnographic museum

Working olive press

La Molienda restaurant

the bars in the Plaza (La Trocha has good local tapas)

Its attractive streets

The Torreon

-

WALK 54 BENALAURIA LAS CANCHAS AND THE TAJO BERMEJO

Time: 2.3 hours (6 kilometres) 3 hours if walk from main road
Difficulty: difficult
Terrain: tracks to begin with then rough rocky paths steep in places, some rock scrambling.

Brief description: a challenging walk with great rewards . The view from the Tajo de Bermeja is worth the effort. You also pass the the hamlet of Las Canchas, before climbing up to the pass of the Hoya Grande then reaching the highest point of any walk in this book at 1137 metres.

HOW TO GET THERE

take the A369 Gaucin to Ronda road and just before the turn off to Benalauria drive up a gravel track on the left , which after 100 metres becomes a concrete track, which heads to the Col de Benalauria along the GR 249.   Park at the top just after the concrete finishes. You can walk up from the A369 and that will add 40 minutes to the walk .

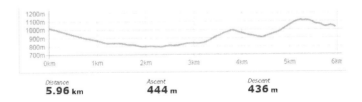

Distance	Ascent	Descent
5.96 km	**444 m**	**436 m**

Mapometer route showing distances in Kilometres
http://gb.mapometer.com/walking/route_4451697.html

Wikiloc link courtesy of Roger Collinson
https://www.wikiloc.com/wikiloc/view.do?id=16303586

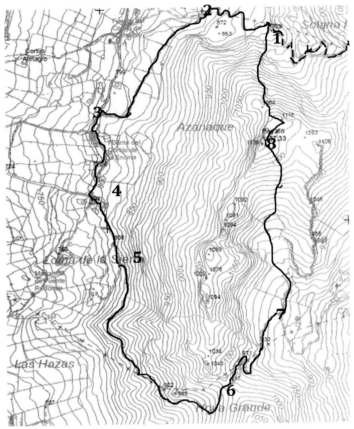

THE WALK

At the pass(MAP 1) (36.598519° -5.279784°) continue
along the track as it heads down the hill west towards the
Guadiaro valley below. There are frequent hairpin bends
and at one there is a spring which has water all year round .
After 20 minutes look for a turn off to the left through a
gate with a red and white cross on the rock . (MAP 2)
(36.600045° -5.287184°) This path passes along a field
between two fences for a few hundred metres before

veering right into trees, losing height and emerging onto a track. (MAP 3) (36.596208° -5.291900°)Turn left and you will pass through the hamlet of Las Canchas where there is a scattering of houses. After passing a spring and trough in a wall on the left and a house with a swimming pool on the right look for a track going up an open grassy area and passing to the right of a house with a blue painted railing on its balcony and a crimson painted gate on the right . (MAP 4) (36.592505° -5.292360°) The track is just before a stone built bench, and a wire and post gate. As it approaches the house it bends to the right, passing a threshing floor and runs along the contour line. Pass through a wire and post gate and after 250 metres from the start of the track look for an obvious path to the left passing through some rocks and a gap in the fence. (MAP5) (36.590033° -5.291033°) Take this path which starts off running parallel to the track and then gradually climbs up and away from the track below. After 400 metres (5 minutes) or so the path splits: take the left fork which heads upwards. The path is not always absolutely distinct. The general direction is upwards and between two sets of impressive rocky crags. Once through the second line of these crags the path then heads into a wide gully, crosses and the bends to the left and then heads upwards towards the gap in the ridge above .

When you arrive here (MAP 6) (36.584921° -5.285936°) head through this pass which has the air of a disused and abandoned quarry. Take the rough track down which is badly eroded in places and after a right and then a left hairpin bend , passing through a rough gate across the track, head for some 300 metres between a few scattered trees . The track makes a turn to the right above a ruin. Look ahead and up the wide valley for a yellowy building

with a radio aerial .(MAP 7) (36.587838° -5.283677°)
Take a faint track going straight on from this corner which
starts to head up the rocky sided valley towards this building
. You pass to the right of a low rock face in front of you just
a couple of metres high. After passing by the yellow hut
you start climbing up the valley and after passing what look
like random stone walls head off to the right through a rock
strewn strewn area towards the top in a more or less
northerly direction. You are looking for a trig point which
has been knocked down and marks the top of the Tajo de
Bermeja or Poyato (1137 metres). The author has placed
single stones on rocks to show the way . It is best to go
slightly right of the summit and approach from the right
hand side . At the top the cliffs go tumbling down very
steeply the other side so be careful here. (MAP 8)
(36.595073° -5.283824°)

When you have admired the views from here towards
Cortes to the west, carry on northwards keeping the cliff to
your left facing a massive cliff face (featured on the cover
of the book) which is above the concrete track on which
you started the walk and clamber down to an open rocky
area where if you are lucky you will find a rough path
marked with cairns heading into scrubby oak trees. Pass
through and look for a fence the other side and a wire gate
tied with blue string. Pass through and head right along the
fence and when you arrive at a ridge going left drop down
(quite steep here) where a fence will appear to your right
and another fence below you. Head to the corner where
these fences meet. There is a gap here. Pass through and
folllow a rough path down the ridge between bushes until
you reach the track where you started the walk.

WALK 55 BENALADID TO BENALAURIA CIRCUIT

Time: 2 hours (5.8 Kilometres)
Difficulty: easy
Terrain: rough paths and track to finish

Brief description: A recently completed section of path now connects Benaladid with Benalauria without having to use the main road. The high return route affords great views up to the Sierra de las Nieves and Upper Genal villages

http://gb.mapometer.com/walking/route_4456312.html

HOW TO GET THERE A 369 Ronda to Gaucin. Drive in main
entrance to village park near the castle (now the cemetery)

Distance	Ascent	Descent
5.83 km	**379** m	**374** m

THE WALK Walk through the village heading south past the
church and the main square. At the far end take a steep

concrete track to the right going up hill past first the sports pitch and then the swimming pool. At the top go left past the swimming pool and take the grassy path going into the trees with the main road just above. Follow this path which has only recently been constructed, as it traverses the slope below the main road.

Eventually it turns left away from the road, crosses a stream bed and rises up to meet a track. There is a display panel here displaying information about a path which you are about to take called Laeras. (MAP 1) (36.600274° -5.266588°) You cross over the track and descend on a well-maintained path which is heading towards Benalauria below you. Turn right at a junction of paths and cross a stream. You will shortly cross a second stream on a tiny bridge.

As you enter the village there is a wash house on the right and then when you come to a concrete ramp go right up the slope and then up some steps to a parking area. Turn left onto Calle Estacion, then a right fork and follow the main street through the village. Then Calle Fuente, passing the town hall on the main square. Near the church at the end of Calle Fuente, turn right up Calle Cruz then left up Calle Alta. Then left along Calle Parras for 70 metres and take a short concrete road off to the right which finishes in a few metres near a sign indicating a path to the right behind the last house to Torreon Mirador. (MAP 2) (36.593044° -5.261956°) Dont go up here but straight on up a narrow path which clings to the side of a steep slope. The path enters a gully with trees. It crosses the bottom of the gully and continues on the other side up the hill and at the top meets a track. (MAP 3) (36.592617° -5.267044°) Go straight over and go down the hill on a track in the same direction. You will pass a couple of houses on the left and a swimming pool on the right before meeting a road.   Turn left, walk 200 metres up the road to a junction. (MAP 4) (36.595072° -5.272724°) Cross over and take the rough track up the slope with waymarks. You join a concrete track which you follow for a few metres before taking a right fork by a finger post indicating the GR 249 to Benadalid.

This rough track will take you all the way back to Benadalid running roughly parallel to and above the main road, although you wont be aware of it until you almost reach Benadalid. During the route you will pass through a gate then start descending (steeply in places) until, after passing a white building on a zigzag, then through a gate, you arrive at a driveable track. Turn right and head down to the road. Turn left on to the road and take the main entrance to the village down which you should find your car.

BENADALID POINTS OF INTEREST

The former castle now cemetery

the narrow picturesque streets .

The Square (a new hotel just below)

WALK 56 – BENADALID TO THE VENTA SAN ISIDORO

Time: 2.5 hours
Difficulty: medium
Terrain : Tracks and paths

Brief Description: This is an impressive walk, easy to navigate, with great views in all directions . A bit of climbing two thirds of the way round is worth the effort and the path down from the pass has been completely cleared in 2017 by the Ayuntamiento of Benadalid.

HOW TO GET THERE Take the A369 Ronda to Gaucin road and when you reach Benadalid take the main street down into the village. Park near the castle now the village cemetery.

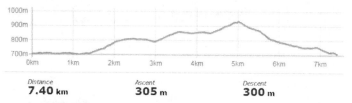

Distance
7.40 km

Ascent
305 m

Descent
300 m

WIKILOC TRACK
https://www.wikiloc.com/wikiloc/spatialArtifacts.do?event=setCurrentSpatialArtifact&id=17887994

THE WALK With your back to the castle facing up the street you came in on, take a track to the right by a warehouse. It is signposted GR 141. (red and white bands) This leads to a picnic area with concrete tables and then contiinues into the countryside. Ignore any entrances or side turnings .

The track eventually turns right into a finca but you continue on what is now a rough track/ wide path and then dwindles to a rough path. There are two forks , on both occasions keep left. After 2 kilometres from the start there is a ruin ahead.

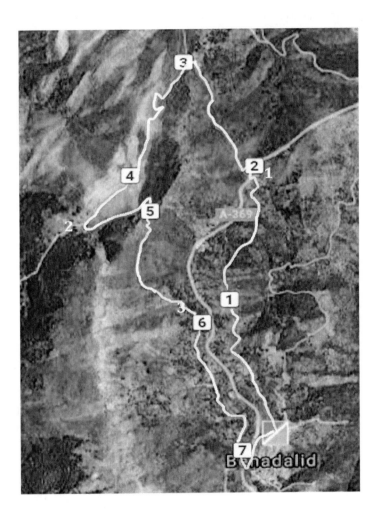

just by the road. Turn sharp left up the bank before the ruin and turn right on to the road. Go 50 metres and turn left up the track opposite this ruin formerly the Venta San Isidoro. (MAP 1) (36.622817°   -5.269971°)

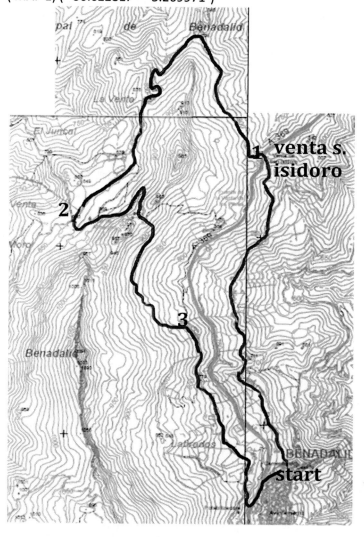

After 1 kilometre you pass a collection of ramshackle huts on the corner as the track turns sharp left and descends. It then rises again after a zigzag and crosses a ridge and there is a farm on the right. On the left there is a new plantation of trees . Your eventual direction is up a path above this plantation. Go past an open water tank on the right and 300 metres past this tank head left up hill by a gate across the track and follow the fence up to a path which is heading left up below the cliffs . (MAP 2) (36.619799° -5.280528°) There is a water trough here with lovely clear water coming from a spring.

The path beomes cobbled in places and after a zigzag, heads through a pass and then heads south back towards Benadalid . There are yellow blobs on the rocks from time to time, but it is an easy path to follow. After ignoring one fork to the right you reach the fence of a smallholding on the right. Keep to the left and you will meet a driveable track at the bottom . (MAP 3) (36.614895° -5.273955°)

Turn right and follow this track all the way back to Benadalid passing a few fincas on the left and right and passing through a wire and post gate. By a pylon ignore a track going right through gates.

The track joins the GR 141 coming down through a gate on the right from Benalauria and reaches the main road opposite a venta. Turn left and the street leading to your car is 150 metres further down on the right.

The author's experience is that the bars are rarely open In Benaladid but it is pleasant to wander the streets.

WALK 57 ATAJATE TO THE CORTIJO DEL TOSTAJAR

Time: 2 hours
Difficulty: Easy
Terrain: Track and path

Brief description: A walk to a remote farmhouse in a spectacular position and returning via the GR 141 A relatively flat walk but with good views.   There may be a gate to climb.

HOW TO GETTHERE   Atajate is on the A369 Ronda to Gaucin road. You need to enter the village and park in the former

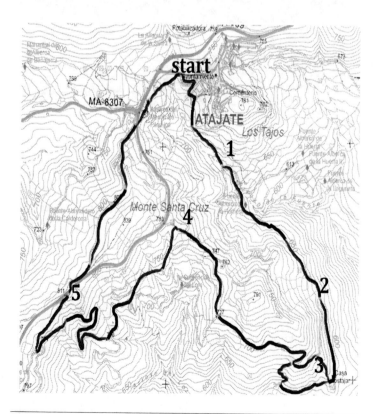

main road through the village near the farmacia at south
end of the village

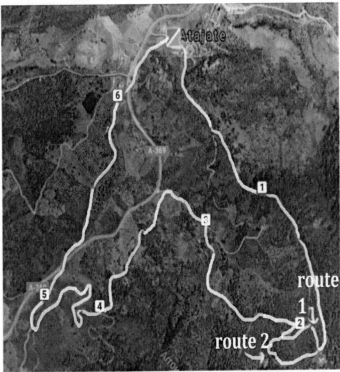

http://gb.mapometer.com/walking/route_4476335.html
Mapometer track showing distances in kilometres and link

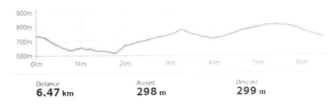

Link to wikilocs to download track courtesy Roger Collinson
https://www.wikiloc.com/wikiloc/view.do?id=16343250

THE WALK

Take the street between the farmacia and the Hostal La Slerra. Pass to the right of a long row of terrace houses then turn left to pass along the front with waste ground on the right. At the end turn right and at the end of the next row of housing turn left. Go 50 metres and by a ruin on the right take a rough track to the right running between walls. Pass through a gate and the path goes down the left side of a gully between trees heading towards the bottom. Go through a bedstead gate and when the path splits just the other side take the right fork, continuing down hill where you will meet a track at the bottom. You enter the track just by a large gate across the track (MAP 1) (36.636635° -5.244669°) Go 30 metres to the left and where the track forks look for a small path to the right of the two tracks. Take this path down the slope to the right.

Folllow this recently cleared path for 15 minutes . It first crosses a stream, rises a little (ignore one path to the left going back down to the stream) to pass by a finca on the left . It passes through two bedstead gates all the time clinging precariously to the side of the hill.   It reaches another bedstead gate which leads to a track which is on a hairpin bend. (MAP 2) (36.631665° -5.238805°)

Turn left and after 5 minutes and ignoring one track to the left you will arrive at a large building on the left of the track. This is the Cortijo del Tostajar. At this point on the right of the track is a water pipe and an improvised water trough made out of an oil drum . There are two ways from here . MAP 3) (36.628530° -5.238080°)

1 scramble up the bank past two water containers and find a rough but clearly defined path heading straight up the ridge. Follow for 5 minutes and you will reach a track. Turn left and head along this track until just before you reach the main Ronda Gaucin road . This is a shorter route but involves a scramble up the bank at the start

2 OR walk for 5 minutes further along the track and when you can see a finca below with a white water tank look for a path going up the bank on a ridge. About 20 metres further on there is a fence on the left of the track. If you reach this fence you have come too far and you need to retrace your steps. Cairns will mark this path which is used by corkcutters. It turns right after only 5 metres and zigzags up through cork trees . Keep on the main path as there are many sideshoots; your aim is to climb upwards, keeping right when you can. After 5 -10 minutes with luck you will reach a track on a hairpin. Turn left .

Keep on this track as it rounds the hill. There is one metal gate which may be closed; it easy to climb over. Carry on until just before you reach the main road having ignored one fork to the left with gates across and noted one track joining from the right.

About 50 metres before the main road by two pylons and at the end of an almond grove on your left there is a grassy track heading down the hill to the left. (MAP 4) (36.634410° -5.247780°) There is also a bedstead gate on the corner at the top of this track. Head down this steep track where at some stages there are landslips on the right hand bank. You will arrive at a gate (may be open). Just after the gate ignore a turn to the left down to a shack then ignore one track up to the right going backwards and then another track going up slightly to the right, making sure you follow the track between trees downhill (there is a plastic water container on the left). You shortly arrive in front of a farm building, go right here and continue down hill until you meet a track after passing through a gate with a polite notice asking you to close the gate. (the sign announcing the fact that the owner is called Antonio del Rio)

Turn right here and follow up hill as it snakes its way towards the main road up above. You meet another wide track which is the GR141 coming from Benadalid to your left and which you will follow back to Atajate. Turn right to complete the last 300 metres before arriving at the main road. (MAP 5) (36.631526° -5.254016°)

Cross over and follow the GR signs (red and white bands on posts) until you meet the main road just before the Venta Las Pilarejos. Cross over and just beyond the venta there is a paved path to the right heading down to the village. Turn right when you reach the road and you will find your car.

Refreshments are on hand at the Hostal la Sierra .

k

WALK 58 ALPANDEIRE LOWER CIRCUIT

Time: 2 hours (5 Kilometres)
Difficulty: easy
Terrain: tracks , short stretch of road, rough path

 Brief description: A straightforward walk to navigate with
a good variety of landscape. Open country , a river valley
and some woodland.

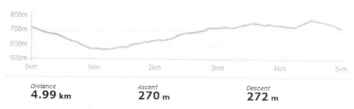

Distance	Ascent	Descent
4.99 km	**270** m	**272** m

Map showing distances in kilometres

http://gb.mapometer.com/walking/route_4457613.html

https://www.wikiloc.com/wikiloc/view.do?id=16814405

HOW TO GET THERE   From the A369 Ronda to Gaucin road take the MA 7307 to Alpandeire. Drive past the village and park at the far end of the village. There is a ramp down to a large area below a wheelie bin collection on the left hand side of the road.

THE WALK Take the last street on the right as you leave the village in the direction of Farajan (Calle de la Plaza). If you have parked near the wheelie bins walk back a few metres and turn left) Pass through the Plaza de Fray Leopoldo and at the bottom take a left fork (MAP 1) (36.632416° -5.202947°) to follow a walled track through open fields. After a gate with a ramshackle farm on the right , there is a sign La Picota on the path you should take. Take a right fork 100 metres further on, then another right fork a further 100 metres later, and follow as the track, then path descends through scattered trees towards the valley floor. At the bottom cross a stream (bed) and keep on the path which meets a driveable track which has crossed the stream from a gate the other side .

Turn left and follow this track which zigzags up the hill through the woods ignoring one turn to the left until you emerge onto a more substantial track which comes up from the right through gates . (MAP 2) (36.622278° -5.203300°)

Turn left and continue up this track ignoring a couple of turnoffs to the right until you reach a tarmac road. This is the Alpandeire to Farajan road. (MAP 3) (36.628850° -5.192231°)

Turn left and go for 500 metres soon curling round a farm above the road and then heading for a rocky hillside in front

of you.   As the road bends round to the left after Kilometre
marker 1 look for a rough path heading up a gap between
the rocky slopes (MAP 4) (36.633072°   -5.194592°) (its
just before a reetaining wall on the right and follow it to
the saddle.   Then edge round to the left across the grass
where you meet a fence which you keep to your right as
you approach a farm below to your right. Join a track
coming from the farm building to the right. Turn left
towards the road and the village below and you will soon
arrive at the road where your car is parked.

OTHER ATTRACTIONS IN ALPANDEIRE

Magnificent church dedicated to Fray Leopold many years
years under restoration

Casa fray Leopoldo

EL POZANCON after heavy rain an underground stream
erupts just below the village

EL CHURRERO a magnificent waterfall further downstream
from the Pozancon

Monument to FRAY LEOLPOLDO . Just above the Farajan
road near the start of the walk

HOTEL Casa grande   a good restaurant and accommodation

It s ancient sinuous streets including a museum

WALK 59 ALPANDEIRE -UPPER CIRCUIT

time: 2 hours (6 Kilometres)
Difficulty: hard due to rough steep terrain
Terrain: tracks , one rough goat path and one section across
a mountainside.

Brief description : A spectacular walk well worth the tough
climb early in the walk to enjoy the views from the upper
track , before gradually descending on this 6 kilometre
circular walk.

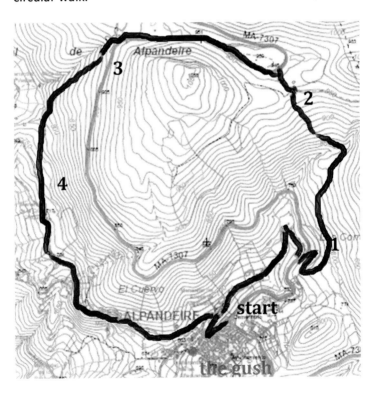

HOW TO GET THERE   From the A369 Ronda to Gaucin road take the MA 7307 to Alpandeire. Park as in Walk 37 and walk back along the road and take the street signposted to the Hotel Casa Grande to the left called Calle Ronda.

Distance	Ascent	Descent
5.97 km	**344** m	**346** m

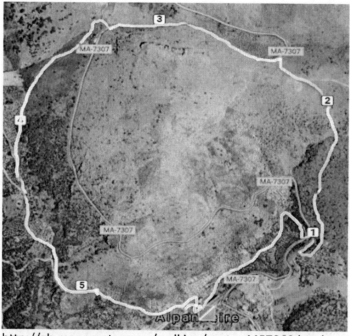

http://gb.mapometer.com/walking/route_4457060.html
https://www.wikiloc.com/wikiloc/view.do?id=16811685

THE WALK   Walk down the street Calle Ronda. As the
street curves round to the left take a steep set of steps
down to the right and turn left at the bottom to pass the
hotel Casa Grande and then turn right on to a road which
leads down to the bottom of the valley floor.

Turn right at the bottom onto a concreted road, which
gradually leads uphill past sheds and stone walls on the left
hand side of the road and a little farmhouse called Yeguada
Piche. The cemented part ends, continue past two white
houses on the left until you reach a tarmac/asphalted road
700m, 15 min from start. Turn left, cross the road and after
20m turn right onto a track uphil.l Pass through a wire gate
and immediately turn 90 degrees left off the track and
head diagonally up the rock strewn slope towards a fence.
A couple of cairns will help point you in the right direction.
When you reach the fence follow it keeping it on your right
and you will come to a gap in a fence running up the hill.
Pass through and continue in the same direction which is
roughly north: there will be more cairns to help you. A
general rule is to follow where the rocks have been stained
brown by sheep and goats over the years.
The path   is very uneven and rocky and known as the
'Vereda Fuentezuela', an old cattle drovers route which
connects to the 'Vereda de Estepona a Encinas borrachas'
higher up. It starts to curve round to the right and you
should look across the gully to your left to spot a large
mound of rubble high above you, It is a paler colour than
than the surrounding rocks.   Until you cross the gully
your direction has been roughly north.
When you cross over the gully turn sharp left and climb
north west uphill towards the previously mentioned mound
of rubble.   The path is vague here but cairns will help , zigzag if you feel it is   too steep.   You need to look out for the

rubble platform as that is your destination. Behind the
platform a wire gate leads on to to a track, at the highest
point of the walk at 963m on the upper 'Vereda', where you
turn left.

You soon arrive at a tarmac road below. Turn left and follow
for just under a kilometre (10 minutes) where the road
curves round to the left . Here turn right through a wire and
post gate then left onto a track and after 50 metres look
for a gap on the fence on the left to find a small path
heading down the hill , intially parallel to the road above,
then moving away.

After another kilometre and entering olive groves join a
more substantial track coming up from the right, you turn
left and follow it round the hill until Alpandeire comes into
sight. Down to the right at the entrance to the village the
streambed emerges from an underground channel under
the village known as the Pozancon (the gush). It activates
after heavy rains. To reach your car you need to cross over
the gully and take one of the streets up towards the hotel
Casa Grande and then back to the road, or take a meander
through the pretty streest of Alpandeire.

WALK 60 FARAJAN -CHORRERAS DE BALASTER

Time: 1. hour
Difficulty: moderate due to very steep climb
Terrain: special paths laid by the town hall and earth tracks

Brief description: This is a short but spectacular walk worth
the detour from the A369 . The town hall has connected
the 2 waterfalls so that from 2016 a circular walk is possible
with a deviation to the second waterfall.

HOW TO GET THERE

Take A 369 Ronda to Gaucin and turn off at K 7 signposted
Alpandeire and Farajan. Farajan is 3 kilometres beyond
Alpandeire. Park at the entrance to the village.

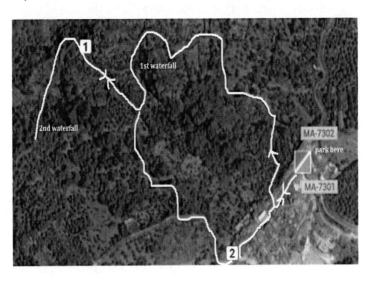

http://gb.mapometer.com/walking/route_4457067.html

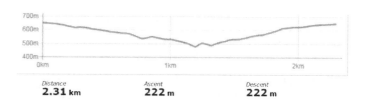

Downloadable GPS track from wikilocs
https://www.wikiloc.com/wikiloc/view.do?id=15149647

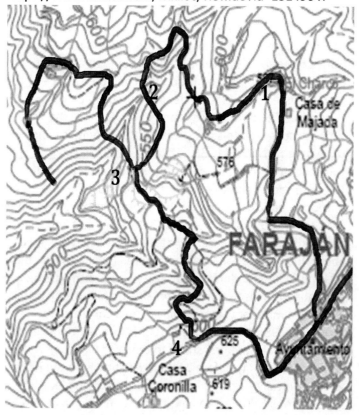

THE WALK Take the street leading to the church and town hall . (Calle Corchuela) Just before the Plaza del Ayuntamiento and opposite Bar Muñoz there is a street turning right . Take this rough concrete track which descends with a wall on the right . Pass one entrance and then a large tree. Then take a left fork indicated by a post with yellow and white flashes.

You then approach an entrance to a finca . (MAP 1) (36.619160° -5.189830°)Turn left just before and follow a concrete path with a small gully in the middle carrying water from a stream. Pass a ruined mill on your left and then the path starts dropping rapidly and the concrete surface of the path has been deliberately deeply scored which will assist your grip. The path bends round to the left and the first waterfall comes into sight (Chorrera 1). There is a picnic table here . (MAP 2) (36.618889° -5.192054°) You now cross the stream with care and follow the path across terracing and then turn sharp right up the slope with a wooden balustrade on your right. You join a wider path . (MAP 3) (36.618275° -5.192236°) Turn right and descend to view the second waterfall (Chorrera 2). It is about 400 metres each way from here. Having returned to this spot you now climb up this very steep path passing several entrances to fincas. After several minutes you will arrive at a mirador (viewing place) on a concrete track. (MAP 4) (36.616513° -5.191158°) Turn left to return to the village. Take the first street to the left (Calle del Molino) which rises steeply before passing the church on the left with (ironically) a plaque on the wall describing local superstitions ! The town hall appears on your right and you continue straight on to rejoin your car.

WALK 61 - JIMERA DE LIBAR TO ESTACION DE JIMERA

Time: 2 hours
Difficulty: easy
Terrain: mainly tracks, village street and rough path

Brief description: A gentle walk between two villages, part of the walk follows the river Guadiaro and the last section climbs up a pretty path

HOW TO GET THERE From A 369 Gaucin to Ronda road turn off at Atajate to Jimera down the MA 8377. Park on the edge of Jimera as the road skirts the foot of the village.

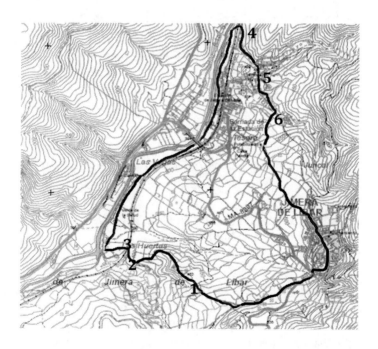

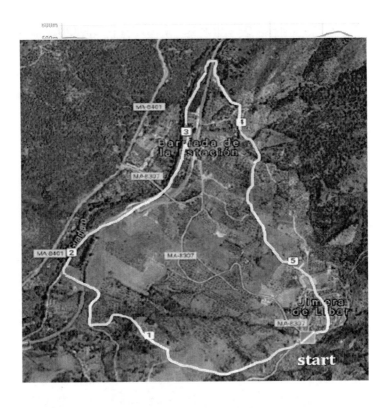

http://gb.mapometer.com/walking/route_4467470.html

https://www.wikiloc.com/wikiloc/view.do?id=16968996
courtesy   Matthew Wolfman

THE WALK walk back up the road towards Atajate passing a water fountain and former wash house on the left. Just after the last building on the right about 100 metres past the washhouse take a track to the right. There is a display board for the GR 249 which you follow for the first part of the walk. Continue along this track for about 15 minutes ignoring one track to the left and and when the main track bends left take the track to the right down the hill. There is a sign post saying Camino Majuelos and a second post with a white arrow. Ignore one track to the right after 50 metres. Pass close by a farm on the left and then the track winds to the left down the hill towards the railway below. At the bottom turn right where you meet a junction of three tracks and follow a track which approaches the railway and then veers away to the right . In 2017 a gate is being constructed a few metres down the track. After 200 metres when you approach a wooden bridge over a small stream turn left just before, down a path which passes alongside a finca amongst bamboos then crosses the railway before arriving at a track.

Turn right onto this track which follows the bank of the River Guadiaro on the left and the railway line on the right before entering the village of Estacion de Jimera, passing under a road bridge. Continue along this street passing the station on the right, a few more buildings and then entering woodland on your right with the river on your left. The street turns into a track and then arrives at a new pedestrian bridge over the railway and meets the path which goes from Jimera to the next village up the valley , Benaojan. Turn right to follow this path back towards Estacion De Jimera .
Pass to the left of a farm on a narrow path, then a track which crosses a stream bed on a bridge when you will arrive at a meeting of several tracks with a bewildering display of walking sign posts. Go straight across leaving a cluster of signposts on your left making sure you have noted one sign indicating the way to Jimera de Libar

1.2 K. (the road back to Estacion de Jimera is to the right)
You are now on a concrete track leading slightly uphill
passing a house on the left. After passing two more fincas
on the right and 400 metres from the start of this track (5
minutes), take a right turn up the hill.   After only 50 metres
the track bends to the right and upwards towards a house,
you go straight on up a rough track/path,
marked by waymark posts one of which tells you that you
are following the Ruta de Fray Leopoldo, (a holy man from
Alpandeire). Ignore a turn into a field after 40 metres,
keeping on the main path up the hill.

Later you pass one house on the right as it enters more
open country and widening before arriving at the village. At
the first road go straight over leaving a sports complex on
your left, and go up into the village past a small hotel on
the left   and then through an archway arriving at the
square with the church on the right. Exit the square to your
left and head down the hill to your car at the bottom on the
main road.

GLOSSARY

Arroyo	stream
Ayuntamiento	town hall
Camino	way / path / route
Cañada	drovers way
Carril	track
Cortijo	farmhouse
Farmacia	chemist
Finca	country property / smallholding
GR	Gran recorrido/ long distance path
Mirador	Viewing place
Plaza	Town square
PR	Pequeño Recorrido / local path
Pueblo	village
Rio	river
Senda / sendero	path
SL	Senda local/ local path
Vereda	wider path

CPSIA information can be obtained
at www.ICGtesting.com
Printed in the USA
LVOW08s1444070817
544123LV00037B/1948/P